LIFE
PREACHING

PRACTICAL ADVICE ON
PREACHING GOD'S WORD

LIFE
PREACHING

PRACTICAL ADVICE ON PREACHING GOD'S WORD

JONATHAN McCLINTOCK

WORD AFLAME PRESS
HAZELWOOD, MO

LIFE PREACHING

PRACTICAL ADVICE ON PREACHING GOD'S WORD

WORD AFLAME PRESS
8855 Dunn Road, Hazelwood, MO 63042
www.pentecostalpublishing.com

Library of Congress Cataloging-in-Publication Data
McClintock, Jonathan, 1973-
Life preaching : practical advice on preaching God's word / by Jonathan McClintock.
pages cm
Includes bibliographical references.
ISBN 978-0-7577-4710-6 (alk. paper)
1. Preaching. I. Title. BV4211.3.M329 2015
251--dc23

2015021060

CONTENTS

FOREWORD 7

INTRODUCTION 9

I. INTRODUCTION TO PREACHING 13

1. WHAT IS PREACHING? 15

2. WHY WE PREACH 27

3. WHAT WE PREACH 41

4. CALLED TO PREACH 55

5. A HIGH AND HOLY CALLING 67

II. SERMON PREPARATION 81

6. WHY I READ SO MUCH 83

7. DECIDING WHAT TO PREACH 93

8. RESEARCHING THE SERMON 105

9. THE IMPORTANCE OF UNDERSTANDING
   THE PASSAGE'S IDEA 115

10. THE IMPORTANCE OF DEVELOPING THE SERMON IDEA .. 125

11. UNDERSTANDING YOUR AUDIENCE 137

12. PRAYER AND THE MESSAGE 145

III. SERMON CONSTRUCTION 155

13. SETTING THE STAGE WITH YOUR INTRODUCTION 157

14. STRUCTURING YOUR MESSAGE FOR GREATEST IMPACT .. 167

15. CREATIVITY 177

16. SELECTING EFFECTIVE ILLUSTRATIONS 183

17. CRAFTING A COMPELLING CONCLUSION 193

18. THE APPLICATION AND CALL TO ACTION 205

IV. SERMON DELIVERY **215**

19. PREACHING WITHOUT NOTES 217

20. PREACHING FROM A MANUSCRIPT 231

21. THE POWER OF PERSONALITY IN PREACHING 239

22. THE ANOINTING 253

V. CONCLUSION **265**

23. LIFE PREACHING 267

APPENDIX 1
THE PHYSICAL SIDE OF PASSION IN PREACHING 275

APPENDIX 2
THE DIFFERENCE BETWEEN TEACHING AND PREACHING .. 281

ENDNOTES 289

BIBLIOGRAPHY 293

OTHER SUGGESTED READING 295

INDEX 297

FOREWORD

Jerry Jones

Jonathan McClintock has written an important book. Preaching is at the heart of the mission of the church because it is integral to both the process of initial salvation, and our developing relationship with God; continuing to inspire and guide us as we journey through this life. Sadly, nowadays preaching is sometimes treated lightly or sometimes minimized, as in statements like: "We need more than just preaching!" or "We need a meeting with less preaching and more teaching." Or as someone once asked me: "Are you just gonna preach or are you going to say something?" But in spite of its detractors, the best thing, the most important thing, and the most effective thing we can do is preach the Word.

Preaching is more than what happens in the pulpit. What happens during preaching is the result of so much more that is mostly behind the scenes. Brother McClintock makes this clear throughout his book, beginning with the title itself. Preaching is the result of living life. Phillips Brooks is credited with the classic definition of preaching, paraphrased in his *Lectures on Preaching:* "Preaching is the communication of Divine truth through human personality." If by "human personality" he meant the sum total of all that makes an individual human being who they are; all the joy and disappointment, success and failure, ups and downs, then he was certainly on the mark. Who we are is forever linked with the ministry we will have, and who we are is the sum of the life we have lived.

Life Preaching never loses sight of this fact. It presents preaching from the human perspective based on interviews with some of the outstanding preachers of our day. The author skillfully introduces the topic with solid commentary, and then illuminates it with the experiences and accumulated wisdom of those who have lived the preacher's life. It is as if you could travel the country and spend time with some of the very best preachers of the Oneness world and learn from them the fundamentals of the most important part of your ministry. This book deserves a place in your library. You will open it again and again and each time will learn something more.

Thank you, Jonathan, your old pastor is proud of you.

INTRODUCTION

I imagine that if most of us took a look at last Sunday's sermon, we could all point out parts that worked well and parts that need some improvement. For some preachers, their introduction was amazing. But after that it is was all downhill. For others, the title was intriguing. But sadly, the content of the sermon failed to deliver on the same creative level as the label it wore. Still other preachers stumbled through the first half of their message, but thankfully, somewhere toward the end, they found their stride and closed it out admirably.

Imagine with me . . . what if we were able to pull all of those "best" elements from all of our sermons and create one great sermon? I don't mean to make this sound trite or like a game. I just know that if you are like me, you sincerely want to improve your preaching. We would love to get behind the pulpit this coming Sunday with power-packed content at each stage of the message. Although a measure of hard work can improve a sermon's content, sometimes even the best content is constructed and delivered poorly.

Poor delivery will cause the audience to drift off and miss out on our key ideas. The hearers need to be challenged at every turn. If the audience is bored and unengaged, it is not their fault; it is our fault. We can blame their limited attention span on our culture of thirty-minute sitcoms and fast-paced video games. Yet in spite of the challenges of preaching today, we must preach a message that will reach this generation.

This book taps into the minds of some of Pentecost's greatest preachers. How and what do they think about preaching? When it comes to their sermon preparation, construction, and delivery, what are their ideas, strategies, and philosophies? What have they found that works best? Think of this book as your ticket to sit in their office, look at their books, hear them develop a thought, pray over their message, construct their notes alongside them, and then stand by their pulpit as they preach with passion the saving gospel of Jesus Christ.

Even though we will thoroughly review their strategies in sermon preparation, we will not seek to break down the preaching process to the extent that it becomes overly academic and void of the Spirit and power. Paul reminds us of the priority of Holy Ghost anointing over "enticing words of man's wisdom" (I Corinthians 2:4). Let us never neglect the unction of the Holy Ghost in our preaching. We must never fear stepping away from our well-crafted sermons to be led of the Spirit and minister to the needs of the congregation. But neither should we neglect the development of our craft.

Preaching goes well beyond proper sermon construction and delivery. The vessel through which the sermon comes will have a major impact on how well the sermon is received. When God called us, He equipped us for the call. This equipping involves more than the talents and abilities gifted to us by our Creator.

He may have equipped you with the ability to tell great stories—an important gift in preaching. But life-changing preaching is more than telling great stories.

He may have equipped you with the ability to speak with tremendous oratory, but life-changing preaching is more than an eloquently delivered speech.

He may have equipped you with the ability to remember facts, figures, and ideas so well that you really don't need a whole lot of notes, but life-changing preaching is more than having a photographic memory.

We tend to elevate storytelling, the gift of oratory, and the ability to preach without notes when we think about the gifts possessed by our favorite preachers. If we were somehow able to draw a picture of the ideal preacher, these abilities, along with several other talents and personality traits, would be sketched with great detail and precision. After the picture is finished, we would step back and admire this well-drawn, neatly constructed, ideal preacher.

But somehow I don't think we would have the picture quite right. Instead, if God were to draw the picture, it would probably look quite a bit different. Instead of being "picture perfect," I imagine that many imperfections would still exist. These defects might actually form the shadow necessary to give the picture life. Look closely and you would see a past filled with the pain of a difficult childhood and the confusion of a teenager struggling to figure out his or her faith. Inner scars from addiction would serve as evidence of God's deliverance. Some would still feel the sting of wounds from the result of mistreatment by a close family member or a knife wound in the back which came from the hand of a close friend. A closer look may reveal haunting memories of abandonment and failure, along with a difficult time where the preacher almost gave up on God because a prayer was not answered as expected. A group of preachers would offer testimony after testimony of how God brought them through it all. The tears, the hurt, the pain, and the victory may actually be the most powerful "abilities" that any preacher brings to the pulpit.

People want to see the wounds that have healed in your life, because they themselves are bleeding, and want to know healing is possible.

This is what *Life Preaching* is all about. We have been called to present ourselves as broken vessels through which God's presence may flow and God's voice may speak.

By showing our scars and telling of our healing, we will be able to meet needs of the congregation.

> The Sunday service is a gathering of troubles. Half of those who enter the church and take their seat before the pulpit are moving in a privatized fog of their own ills. Sunday's single hour of God-talk does not last long enough to lure them back into the world where the sermon would have them live . . . Given the choice they would never choose to be mummified in the bandages of their own ills. They want to be free, and that's partly why they first came to church. They are usually too

fogged to care about when Leviticus was written or whatever happened to the Hittites. They are the wounded, reaching out to snare the God-words that fly at them between 11 and 12 o'clock . . . They are pew-sitters, trying to remain anonymous, while they cry out to the sermonizer, "Hey look! I'm here! I'm bleeding!" They do not want us to bring a set of ancient commentaries against the injuries of their heart. They just want a counselor to stop the hemorrhaging of their souls, and if that can't be done they would like some life-survivor to show them a set of well-healed scars so they can leave the service believing that healing is possible.[1]

Therefore we must preach a message of transformation. What are some areas of your life God has transformed? What are some areas God is in the process of transforming? When you preach from a place of transformation, you are communicating a life-changing message that has been filtered through your own life experience and has been processed more than some other sermons you might study over a two to three week period. These messages preached out of your life are much more meaningful to you, and that passion and conviction will be felt by the audience listening to your burden.

I

INTRODUCTION TO PREACHING

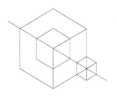

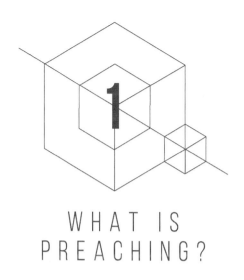

WHAT IS
PREACHING?

"That'll preach!" How many times in your circle of preacher friends has someone made that statement regarding something that was said or a clever thought someone expressed? What is really meant by that exclamation? Consciously or subconsciously there are those who think good preaching consists mainly of a passionate discourse built around a witty or clever thought or a unique take on a verse no one has considered before. Perhaps we are a little confused about what preaching really is. The word for preaching in the New Testament (*kērussō*) means "to proclaim, to herald." Jesus used this word while standing in a synagogue when reading from the prophet Isaiah.

"The Spirit of the Lord is upon me, because he hath anointed me to *preach* the gospel to the poor; he hath sent me to heal the brokenhearted, to *preach* deliverance to the captives, and recovering of sight to the blind, to set at liberty them that are bruised" (Luke 4:18, emphasis mine).

Jesus launched His ministry by declaring His purpose was to preach. He came to proclaim the good news and to herald the message of the kingdom. Jesus can be seen in the Gospels traveling from town to town, standing in the public places, proclaiming to all who would hear, "Repent: for the kingdom of heaven is at hand" (Matthew 4:17). Jesus picked up right where John the Baptist left off.

Desiring to pass the ministry of preaching on to the next generation, Paul wrote to the young pastor Timothy, reminding him that his calling and purpose was to "Preach the Word."

"*Preach* the word; be instant in season, out of season; reprove, rebuke, exhort with all longsuffering and doctrine" (II Timothy 4:2, emphasis mine).

Paul wanted Timothy to realize the importance and power of preaching. "Preaching is more than teaching. It is exultation in the Word. 'Preach the Word,' means 'exult in the Word.' That is, announce it and revel in it. Speak it as amazing news. Speak it from a heart that is moved by it."[2]

When we preach the Word under the direction and unction of the Holy Spirit, something supernatural takes place. We partner with God Himself to herald the truth in love to the hearers.

First and foremost, preaching is the declaration of God's Word.

If you are not preaching God's Word, you are not preaching. If you are "preaching" from the latest leadership book, you are not really preaching. Books can give us great ideas and insight that at times are beneficial to our congregations. But if you are simply spouting information about becoming a better leader without proclaiming principles rooted in a scriptural foundation, you are not preaching; you are giving a book report.

In response to the pressure of trying to keep up with the popular preachers of podcast fame, many ministers have turned their sermons into motivational speeches aimed at informing their congregations on best investment practices, how to increase intimacy at home, and having a positive mindset. Sure, these messages may include some scattered references to the Bible, but only enough to calm their critics. A recent message at a popular megachurch was entitled, "A New Year, A New Song: Experiencing Life through the Elements of Music." For music lovers, it was probably an interesting speech. It probably wasn't preaching.

Many of these churches may as well hand out popcorn before the preacher begins the sermon so that their congregations can sit back and let their ears be itched. Sadly, this shift in the culture of preaching is being felt in Apostolic circles. Calvin Miller wrote about such a shift in culture: "Because the secular culture didn't want a Lord, preaching quit saying, 'Thus saith the Lord.' Now far too few pulpits inform the world that God has something to say to it. In the absence of God's Word, 'how-to' has replaced 'repent and be baptized.'"[3]

"How to" speeches focus on an individual's ideas and not the message of the Master. If it is just your opinion, it is not preaching. Preaching has no room for opinions. The town crier who is sent by the king to stand in the town square, unroll the scroll, and herald the message of the king is not given the latitude to interject commentary of personal opinion. He was sent to sound a clear call from the king.

We are called to preach the Word of God in the twenty-first century. We must make practical applications so people understand how the Scripture relates to their lives. However, we stand on a platform, not a soapbox. All of us have opinions and at times will interject them when we are speaking. But opinions take away from the power of preaching. Opinions are important in the private conversations between pastor and saint, when the saint desires the pastor's opinion on a decision they are considering. But we must be careful when and how personal views are expressed in our preaching.

Preaching is not conversing or discussing. Great benefits can be derived from group discussion. Youth, twenty-somethings, and thirty-somethings love sitting in groups and sharing opinions, questions, and personal ideas. In fact, if you teach these age groups, it would certainly be wise to include discussion time in your small group or class. However, this type of communication is not preaching. Preaching does not ask for feedback in the form of questions or discussion. Of course, this idea flies in the face of popular church culture.

Small groups, Sunday school classes, Bible studies, and fellowship groups provide more than enough opportunities for questions, discussions, and group interaction. But preaching, in the classical sense, has no room for it. Perhaps this is why a number of present-day preachers are arguing for a change:

"Some church leaders recently have argued for a modification of our idea of preaching. For one person to address a host of others in a long monologue, they argue, is simply wrong. It is tyrannizing, depersonalizing, and dehumanizing, a vestige of the Enlightenment or of Hellenistic thinking that we have long since gotten past."[4]

We know this argument to be false. The idea of one man or woman speaking while others listen is truly a powerful representation of God's grace and the salvation He gives to us as a free gift. The act of preaching is symbolic of Jesus Christ standing before humanity offering Himself as the Answer to all of humanity's woes.

Nothing can take the place of the public reading of Scripture and the proclamation of the Word. We have added an awful lot of activity into our services, and most of it is good and worth the time and attention we give it. But let us never lose the act of preaching in our churches.

Singing cannot take the place of preaching. Scripture does not say that God chose the foolishness of music to save them that believe. Music simply sets the stage. You may ask, "What about those times when we have several services in a row where worship is so powerful during the singing and prayer time that the preacher doesn't get a chance to preach? Does that mean that at times the church doesn't need preaching?" I don't think we can make that leap. I believe those times happen as sovereign moves of God that serve as a supplement to faithful preaching. Preaching sows the Word and sometimes it takes time for the seed to germinate, take root, and begin to sprout in people's lives.

From my experience in ministry, I can say that churches trained to value the importance of preaching were the liveliest, the most worshipful, and the most powerful. God honors His Word and those who value the preaching of that Word.

Sadly, some churches have neglected to appreciate the power of preaching.

> The empty pulpit in many of our church buildings well displays the spiritual reality. We run around seeking life for our churches and life for ourselves through a million different methods, and the one means God has given for bringing people into a relationship with Him stands neglected and disdained. In the act of preaching—a congregation hearing the voice of one man who stands behind the Scriptures— God has given us an important symbol of the fact that we come into relationship with Him by His Word . . . we as Christians are made God's people by believing God and trusting His promises. In a word, we come into relationship with God through faith, and "faith comes," Paul tells us in Romans 10, "from hearing, and hearing through the word of Christ."[5]

Peter standing on the balcony of the upper room and heralding the gospel was an anointed display of true preaching. Preaching is imperative. The gospel must be preached. The Word of God must be declared. Powerful preaching must be on display in our pulpits.

Preaching is a divine function accomplished through men and women. Noah was a preacher of righteousness (II Peter 2:5). Solomon was a preacher (Ecclesiastes 1:1, 12). Paul was ordained as a preacher (I Timothy 2:7). The apostle Paul named several women in his letter to the Romans who were instrumental in the operation of the church. Phebe was a deacon (Romans 16:1, NIV). Priscilla was actually mentioned before Aquila in Romans 16:3, and both were recognized for the church that met in their house. Romans 16:12 mentions three other women who "laboured much in the Lord." Each of these women were integral to the churches and the growth of the gospel in that day. We have no direct statement from Scripture that says any of them preached the Word, but it is logical to assume they may have.

As Paul told the Galatian church, "there is neither male nor female; for you are all one in Christ Jesus" (Galatians 3:28, NKJV). This verse is not calling for a removal of being distinctively male or distinctively female in the church. Rather, Paul affirms that we are all part of one body, one people, and one church. Though there may be distinctions in gifts operating in the church (I Corinthians 12, 14), no one should be excluded from preaching the Word of the Lord because of gender.

Some denominations hold a strong stance against women in a preaching role. However, I am happy the Apostolic church has historically promoted and encouraged women to respond to God's call on their lives to preach. My grandmother was widely respected as a wonderful, God-fearing preacher of the gospel. The legacy she left behind is something I am truly thankful for.

God ordained preaching will be accomplished through men and women who have surrendered to the call. He chooses to speak through human preachers declaring, "Thus saith the Lord."

Preaching is God's chosen method. God could have chosen many different means of offering salvation to mankind. Instead, He chose preaching—"the foolishness of preaching." "For after that in the wisdom of God the world by wisdom knew not God, it pleased God by the foolishness of preaching to save them that believe" (I Corinthians 1:21).

A one-on-one conversation can be a powerful experience that God uses to ignite the hunger of a lost soul. A home Bible study is an invaluable tool God has used to flow through a Spirit-led believer and expound truth to people searching for answers in their lives. In fact, a form of preaching may take place in each of those instances. However, biblical preaching, the kind of preaching referred to in I Corinthians 1:21, specifically refers to persuasive speaking in which one man or woman proclaims the gospel of Jesus Christ and the truth of God's Word.

When viewed through the lens of human understanding and intellect, preaching does seem a bit foolish. However, when seen through the eyes of faith, biblical preaching is powerful. Crowds can be moved to tears at one moment, and laughter at the next, when eloquent speeches are delivered. Some of the most affecting speeches I have listened to are TED Talks. They have moved me emotionally and intellectually, but nothing happened spiritually. Those speeches in no way altered my eternal destiny.

However, I have sat under the voice of an anointed preacher, declaring God's promises and power, and was not only moved emotionally and intellectually, but I was also moved to change my ways. Maybe a really incredible speech could motivate me to change my ways, but the speech itself will not be grounded in anything that could assist me in that change. Change on my own is futile. But the preached Word of God, when coupled with my faith, connects me to a Source that is willing and able to help me change. Something happens in the Spirit during biblical preaching that does not and cannot take place during a secular speech.

Preaching . . . Foolish? Sure, but only when you refuse to listen and respond in faith to what is being preached.

I do admit, with a little hesitance, I have heard preaching that was not very beneficial. And looking around at my fellow congregants, it did not appear I was the only one suffering through the abundance of word crutches (e.g., "uh," "praise God," "amen") used by the preacher and the twisting maze of his thought process. We are called to preach—to emphatically and clearly proclaim God's Word. Preaching must be effective.

First of all, in order to be effective, it must be biblically and doctrinally sound. It is not my personality or your personality that makes preaching effective. The Word of God makes it effective. Knowing the truth sets people free. We have a responsibility as preachers to make sure our sermons are biblically and doctrinally accurate. We do not have the liberty of choosing a text and then creating a message explaining that text, when we really have no clue if that is what the author meant or not. In fact, some preachers don't even worry about context. They had a thought, and on the surface, this one verse in the middle of the chapter appears to back up what they are thinking. So . . . that is what it must mean. (We will look at the importance of context in a few chapters.)

One of the fastest ways to lose credibility in your preaching is to continually take Scripture out of context. To be effective, our preaching must be biblically sound. It also must be clearly communicated.

It doesn't matter how good the content of your sermon is or how revelatory the meat of the message will be if those in the audience have a difficult time understanding what you are trying to say. *How you say*—in many cases—is just as important as *what you say*. Often we think we are being clear when we really are not.

Have you ever tried to talk with someone who did not speak English? Just about everyone does the same thing. When we realize they are not getting what we are saying, we usually start talking louder and slower. It really is hilarious to watch. The individual is not hard of hearing; they just do not speak your language. It does not matter how good or how important the message is you are trying to tell them. If you cannot speak their language, pace and volume do not matter.

Some preachers think that speaking loudly is an effective tool for getting the message across. Sometimes, however, a preacher's voice has volume, but it lacks true passion. Preachers need to be fervent to show the importance of the message. If you do not believe what you are saying, do not expect your congregation to believe it either. Passion is felt. Passion can be seen in your eyes, heard in your voice, and felt in the conviction of your delivery. If you are not passionate about what you are going to preach, get back on your knees until you are baptized with passion.

Passionless preaching can even take the wind out of the sails of God's Word. No, it doesn't sap the power from Scripture, but it sure makes it harder for people to look past you. We must never become a barrier between those coming to hear the Word and the Word itself. We must realize we are part of the message being preached. Anything we do to distract from the message pulls their attention away from God's Word.

Finally, for preaching to be effective it must be captivating. We have no excuse to not be interesting. I have heard many teachers and preachers complain about the lack of attention given to them by classes and groups they have addressed. In response, these communicators often blame the audience and wonder why they are unable to pay attention for a mere 30-45 minutes. I would propose, if the audience is not actively engaged with the message you are delivering, it is not their fault. As the preacher, you are responsible for delivering the message in such a way that the attention of the hearer is captured and that they stay with you on that 30-45 minute journey.

The individual who is serious about his or her calling to preach must have at least two goals: to become a sound expositor and to become a strong communicator.

Becoming a good preacher is synonymous with being able to adequately explain Scripture (a sound expositor). Paul told Timothy, "Study to shew thyself approved" (II Timothy 2:15). Don't preach something you have not adequately studied out. The last thing you want to do is get into a Bible narrative you spontaneously reference in the middle of your message and then not know the details of the story. Such a situation can be not only embarrassing, but it can also kill momentum. Equally disappointing is beginning to tell a story referenced in your notes, only to discover that there are several details you just don't know because you didn't take time to really study it out.

We are without excuse in either instance. First of all, if you don't know a story, don't tell it even if it pops in your mind and you think it might illustrate your point well. You will end up losing credibility with your audience when they find out, you, the preacher, don't know the Bible.

Secondly, if you plan to reference a Bible narrative, take time to study out the details. People can tell when you haven't processed what you are trying to preach. All of us have at least once, picked up a ready-made lesson and jumped into teaching it without adequate preparation. You remember that feeling of stumbling over the content, and you wondered if the audience picked up on your lack of preparation. Let me be honest with you . . . they picked up on it before you realized you were bombing!

As preachers, we need to study consistently, on a regular basis, so we are ready to preach "in season and out of season." There may come a time when you are thrust into the role of preaching and you weren't expecting it. Though this won't happen very often, I do believe that in these instances God will intervene and equip you to draw from those reserve wells you have been digging in your personal time with the Lord.

Our consistent preparation will aid us as we preach on a regular basis. It is our job as preachers to know the Bible. It is our job as preachers to be prepared. Preaching is an act of spiritual warfare. We cannot enter the arena where souls are being fought for and halfheartedly offer a few thoughts on God. We must enter our pulpits with passion, boldness, and confidence. We must be able to pull out a Sword we have tested and rely on a faith that has consistently withstood opposition.

Good preaching doesn't just happen. People are not great communicators because they have a microphone in their hand. Good communicators take their craft seriously. They take time to learn what works and what doesn't. Preaching, at least doing it well, takes a lot of hard work. But why shouldn't we—those called to deliver the life-giving Words of Jesus Christ—work as hard as we can to make sure we are doing it right and doing it well. God expects it. The world and the church deserve it.

What are three things a preacher can begin doing today to improve their preaching?

1. In whatever format you want, keep a journal of your thoughts. We lose way more good thoughts than we should. If I get a thought, I want to be able to write it down immediately.

2. Interact with preaching and teaching. Listen to it. Pay attention to it. Watch not only what he or she (the preacher) says, but how it is said . . . how the passion comes across. Studying preaching is important.

3. To this, add a life of devotion to your craft. If you really feel called to do this and if you are going to do this, you have to give yourself to this. This is not a part-time thing because you have this preaching bent. This either is you and your life or it is not. You don't do this part-time. You don't do this because you think it is something you may be good at. You can't teach leadership without doing the hard work of leading, failing, succeeding, and revising. You can't teach submission unless you have had the chance to rebel. Lock it in your spirit: this is my life and my calling. It's got to be morning, noon, and night. God has to have the permission to teach you at any moment so that you can become the conduit for this to other people.

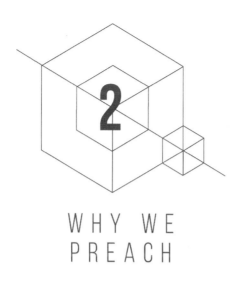

WHY WE
PREACH

"For whosoever shall call upon the name of the Lord shall be saved. How then shall they call on him in whom they have not believed? and how shall they believe in him of whom they have not heard? and *how shall they hear without a preacher?*" (Romans 10:13-14, emphasis mine).

A Chinese farmer, who was nearly blind due to the many cataracts on his eyes, stumbled upon a Christian medical mission. The missionary doctor told the man he could help him see clearly again. After the surgery the farmer was amazed at his restored sight and left the mission full of joy and purpose. Seven days later, as the doctor was finishing breakfast and peering through his kitchen window at the bright blue summer sky, he noticed the formerly blind man holding the front end of a long rope. Following behind him were several blind men and women holding to the rope in a single-file line.

These men and women were people the farmer had told about his operation and the restoration of his sight. They had all heard the farmer tell them the good news of how he had been blind but now could see. He had shared with them the story of the Christian mission and the doctor who had cured his blindness. He was not able to fully explain to them the physiology of the eye or even the technical details of the surgery. He could simply express with excitement and conviction that he once was blind, the doctor had operated on him, and now he was able to see. And this is why they came with him. They wanted the same cure the farmer had experienced.

And this is why we preach. Those of us who once were blind but have received healing by the hand of the Great Physician, have a message to take to this world—a world full of blind men, women, and children. If we do not tell them, they may never find the Doctor on their own.

God's Chosen Method

Preaching is God's chosen method for reaching the lost. When the Israelites rebelled and teetered on the brink of apostasy, God sent them preacher after preacher. When the Ninevites were facing destruction, God sent them a preacher. When David sinned and found himself at odds with God, God sent him a preacher. When Israel needed to be prepared for the coming of the Messiah, God sent them a preacher in the wilderness. When a good man, a praying man, a man hungry for more of God, sought God continually for answers, God sent Cornelius a preacher.

God can and does speak to people through His Word, a still small voice, circumstances, situations, and other means of communication. But when it comes to telling the gospel message, God sends preachers.

When we consider our motivation as preachers, we must make sure it aligns with the reasons God instituted preaching. God chose preaching as the primary avenue for delivering His message of hope to the world. Preaching is not a man-made invention. Preaching is not something man dreamed up so that he or she could claim to speak for God. That would be presumptuous. If it were not God's idea, then so-called preachers would be usurping the authority that had never been given to them.

However, this is not the case. Instead, God decided that the idea of one man or one woman standing before a gathering—small or large—of people and expressing His love for mankind was His preferred method of communication. This is His doing. This is His plan. This is His idea.

In the Old Testament there were times when God declared His Word and promises Himself (e.g., Abraham and Moses). However, His chosen method, even in the Old Testament was always preaching:

"Long ago, at many times and in many ways, God spoke to our fathers by the prophets" (Hebrews 1:1, ESV).

In the New Testament—after the birth of the church—God established preaching as the sole vehicle for delivering His gospel. When the Lord knocked Saul off of his horse by a blinding light, He told Saul to find a preacher named Ananias. God could have explained everything to Saul by Himself, but preaching was the method for the message.

The Catalyst for Faith

"But *without faith* it is impossible to please him: for he that cometh to God must believe that he is, and that he is a rewarder of them that diligently seek him" (Hebrews 11:6, emphasis mine).

No one can come to God without faith. Truthfully, no one will want to come to God without faith. Faith opens the eyes of the searching to see if there is an answer to all of their questions. Faith causes people to see the possibility of things they have hoped for. (See Hebrews 11:1.) Faith gives people the ability to believe God can do what His Word says He will do.

"So then faith comes by hearing, and hearing by the Word of God" (Romans 10:17, NKJV).

True biblical faith is non-existent where the Word of God is not being spoken, taught, or preached. People will never believe on Jesus Christ as their Savior unless they first hear the promise of redemption through the declaration of God's Word. The preaching of the Word ignites faith in the hearts of the hearers.

When the faith of your congregation is low, preach the Word.

When a miracle is needed and people are struggling to believe, preach the Word.

When families are falling apart and people are struggling to hold on, preach the Word.

When young people are wavering because of the alluring nature of sin, preach the Word.

"For whatsoever is born of God overcometh the world: and this is the victory that overcometh the world, even our faith" (I John 5:4).

To overcome, we must have faith. To build an overcoming church, there must be faith. To see God do the miraculous, faith must be present. So when faith cannot be found, preach the Word. Those who hear the proclamation of the Word of God will find faith (Romans 10:17).

When Peter and John were grilled about the circumstances surrounding the healing of the lame man (Acts 3), Peter preached to the crowd about Jesus. This message ignited faith in many of the hearts who heard it.

"Howbeit many of them which heard the word believed . . ." (Acts 4:4).

I cannot help but believe that not only did the preached Word have such an impact on the people because of the nature of the Word—that it was truth and divinely inspired— but it cut deep because these men had spent time with Jesus. (See Acts 4:13.) The Word has weight in and of itself. The

Word can stand on its own merit. But when men and women who have walked with Him, talked with Him, learned from Him, and observed Him at work in their own lives, begin declaring the saving power of the gospel, people will have faith and trust in God.

Acts 8 tells us that Philip went down to the city of Samaria to preach. As he preached the gospel and healed many in the crowd who were sick, the people began listening even more intently to what he had to say. We do not know how he designed his sermon. We know nothing of his delivery or his use of illustrations. All we know from Scripture is that he "preached Christ unto them" (Acts 8:5). And he preached "the things concerning the kingdom of God and the name of Jesus Christ" (Acts 8:12). And when he preached this gospel, they believed and "were baptized, both men and women" (Acts 8:12).

For faith to sprout in the hearts of people, the gospel must be preached.

The Facilitator of Salvation

"For I am not ashamed of the gospel of Christ, for *it is the power of God to salvation* for everyone who believes, for the Jew first and also for the Greek" (Romans 1:16, NKJV).

"For by grace you have been saved through faith. And this is not your own doing; it is the gift of God" (Ephesians 2:8, ESV).

Since we are saved by grace through faith, and preaching the gospel ignites faith in the hearts of the hearers, then we must understand that preaching is the vehicle that brings salvation to mankind. Preaching introduces the sinner to the Savior. Preaching persuades the sinner to respond to the invitation of the Savior and obey the gospel.

After Cornelius saw a vision and heard the Lord tell him to call for Peter, he gathered together his relatives and close

31

friends to hear the man of God speak to them. They waited together until Peter arrived a few days later. When Peter walked into the home, he saw the large group and knew God had called him to preach to these people. Peter proceeded to preach the gospel, telling of Jesus' death and resurrection.

And while Peter preached, salvation came to the house of Cornelius.

"While Peter was still speaking these words, the Holy Spirit came on all who heard the message. The circumcised believers who had come with Peter were astonished that the gift of the Holy Spirit had been poured out even on Gentiles. For they heard them speaking in tongues and praising God." (Acts 10:44-46, NIV).

As we—preachers of the gospel—stand before those who are bound in sin, we hold in our hands the keys to unlock their prison doors. The preached Word of God is able to accomplish more in a few minutes than counseling can in a few years. When preaching ignites faith, faith leads people to experience salvation. The process of salvation creates new creatures—"old things are passed away, behold, all things are become new" (II Corinthians 5:17).

And this is why we preach.

We Preach for Effect

We preach because we desire to see change—change in the lives of our church, our community, and our world.

The message the disciples preached was seeking "not just to invite people to think on a few things, to meditate on this or that idea, or to give a bit of food for thought. It was a message that was aiming for change."[6]

The message we are called to preach is countercultural.

Some things from Scripture will be easy to preach because they will naturally resonate with culture. What we have come to call the "Golden Rule," though not always practiced by business, media, or Hollywood, is accepted and taught by parents to their children. Many people don't know it comes from the Bible; but nonetheless, this idea is widely accepted and practiced in our world.

However, other messages from Scripture often fly in the face of culture: "Whosoever will be great among you, shall be your minister" (Mark 10:43). "If any man will come after me, let him deny himself, and take up his cross, and follow me" (Matthew 16:24). "Let no corrupt communication proceed out of your mouth" (Ephesians 4:29). Although some ideas from the Bible will be acceptable and not find much resistance, the majority of the message we are called to preach is countercultural.

That being said, we should not be surprised when we are not lauded as heroes by the masses. In fact, if you are not being attacked by natural or supernatural forces, you may want to make sure what you are preaching is lining up with the Word of God. Now, we must be wise and speak the truth in love. Just because our message is countercultural does not mean we go looking for fights—that is prideful. We don't parade ourselves as God's gift to humanity and look down our noses on those who are lost in sin.

I was both confused and embarrassed as a teenager when I saw, through the media, a man and his boys standing on a street corner telling everyone who passed by they were going to hell. When interviewed, this man was full of hatred and in no way reflected the godly preachers I grew up listening to. Sidewalk preachers like this man do nothing but disparage the true message of the gospel and leave people convinced that what they thought about Christians is actually true: judgmental and haughty.

We preach for effect. We preach so people are changed. The anointed Word can cut to the heart and convict the listener of their sin. Let the message, not your attitude do the cutting on their hearts.

We Preach to Edify

Paul told the Corinthians that one of his chief concerns was that "everything must be done so that the church may be built up" (I Corinthians 14:26, NIV). Another translation says "Let all these things be done for the strengthening of the church" (NET).

We are called to preach so that we may inform and instruct the church. When a preacher handles the Word of God correctly, the church is educated concerning what God requires of each child of God. In addition to what God requires and expects, God also has blessings and benefits that are to be experienced. The preacher is to adequately expound upon these gifts so the body of Christ is built up.

"All scripture is breathed out by God and profitable for teaching, for reproof, for correction, and for training in righteousness" (II Timothy 3:16, ESV).

So how should we pray for the preaching of the Word to edify our congregations?

"When you preach, the Scriptures will teach, reprove, correct, and train in righteousness."[7]

The Scripture is profitable for doctrinal instruction (positively and negatively) and for ethical instruction (positively and negatively). We all need to be taught how to mesh the Bible and our Christian life. We need preaching and teaching to show us how to grow (positive). But we also need to be shown the error of our ways at times and how our lives are running contrary to God's Word (negative).

The first two words Paul uses are doctrine (teaching) and reproof. When the Scriptures are taught, they are explained so the congregation understands what they are really saying in order to comprehend the meaning the author intended. When the Bible is communicated correctly, the listener will know what is true about God—His character and His ways.

You will only find the word "reproof" used once in the New Testament. Paul was undoubtedly familiar with the way Greek literature presented this term. To the Greeks, this word was used to express strong disapproval. Reproof means "to confront and show the falsehood of wrong ideas about God and His ways."[8] "The second set of words Paul used here, correction and training in righteousness, refer primarily to ethical concerns. Part of edifying a congregation involves teaching them what it means to live in accord with the Gospel."[9] This involves practical instruction and application so that the listener knows how to apply what is found in God's Word.

Correction is the counterpart to reproof. Whereas reproof is used to show the importance of contesting doctrinal error, correction is used to help the Christian develop godly character and Christ-like behavior.

Training in righteousness has somewhat of a parental theme attached to it. Paul often used the idea of coming up into maturity as a metaphor for Christian growth. The idea of a child growing into adulthood is seen in Paul's writings to both the Corinthians and Ephesians.

"Brothers and sisters, stop thinking like children. In regard to evil be infants, but in your thinking be adults" (I Corinthians 14:20, NIV).

"So that we may no longer be children, tossed to and fro by the waves and carried about by every wind of doctrine, by human cunning, by craftiness in deceitful schemes" (Ephesians 4:14, ESV).

We Preach to Evangelize

Take some time to look at your message from the perspective of an unbeliever. Ask yourself, "Will they understand what I am saying?" Too often we gloss over stories from Scripture with the disclaimer, "I know we are all familiar with the story of . . . , so I will not take time to tell that story." Maybe we need to cut some things out of our messages so we can tell that story. You may be surprised at how many saints really don't know that story. Don't shy away from the things you would consider elementary. Even those concepts and stories can be delivered in such a way as to not offend the saint or alienate the sinner.

Before sending His disciples into the surrounding towns and villages, Jesus told them, "and as ye go, preach, saying, the kingdom of heaven is at hand" (Matthew 10:7). There must be a thread of pronouncement in every message we preach—"the kingdom of heaven is at hand." No matter the aim of our message, there must be anticipation for the coming of the Lord and the completion of all things.

There are two aspects of the Lord's coming that should be focused on. First of all, the Lord has come for that congregation, at that moment, and He is present to save, heal, and deliver. Secondly, we should turn the attention of our congregations to the imminent return of Christ for His church. Whether these ideas are specifically addressed or not in every sermon, the attitude and tenor of our messages should point to the coming of Lord.

Not only should our messages proclaim the Lord's coming, but every sermon should be evangelistic. This does not mean every sermon should revolve around Acts 2:38. In fact, if every sermon you preach is only telling people how to respond to the gospel, then you are not truly preaching evangelistically.

For sermons to be evangelistic, they should be Christ-centered and Cross-centered. What did Peter preach on the Day of Pentecost? He started with Joel's prophecy concerning the Spirit and then preached the gospel: Christ's death, burial, and resurrection. What did Peter preach to the crowd gathered at Solomon's Porch in Acts 3? He preached the gospel and the power of Jesus' name. What did Philip preach to the Samaritans in Acts 8? "He preached Christ unto them" (Acts 8:5). What was the subject of Saul's first message after his conversion? "And straightway he preached Christ in the synagogues, that he is the Son of God" (Acts 9:20).

The single thread that ran throughout every message the disciples and apostles preached was the gospel: that Jesus died, was buried, and rose again. It was the gospel that produced conviction in the hearts of the hearers. I find it interesting that the words found in Acts 2:38 did not appear to be a part of Peter's impromptu message.

When Peter stepped to the balcony of the upper room in response to the questions of the crowd, Peter did not immediately jump to: "Let me tell you want you need to do. Repent and be baptized in Jesus' name, and you will receive the Holy Ghost." For some reason we often feel compelled to go there first, and unfortunately we fail to preach the gospel.

When Peter began preaching, he first laid a foundation regarding the prophecies concerning Jesus. Once he had established enough scriptural credibility to prove Jesus was the Messiah, He turned to the guilt of the crowd. "Therefore let all the house of Israel know assuredly, that God hath made that same Jesus, whom ye have crucified, both Lord and Christ" (Acts 2:36).

I wonder how long his pause was after speaking those words. Perhaps the crowd immediately responded. Or just maybe that was the end of Peter's message and for a few moments there was silence.

Imagine with me, if that were to happen today . . .

Peter would have closed his Bible and called for the musicians to come. And as those last few words fell from his lips—"God hath made that same Jesus, whom ye have crucified, both Lord and Christ"—conviction fell down heavy on the hearts of the congregation. Each eye was fixed on

37

Peter. Tears were streaming down some of their faces. Men and women across the crowd were gripping the backs of their pews, stirred in their hearts, but not knowing what to do.

Then somewhere from the back of the audience, a little old man who had lived a long time and whose body was prematurely aged from the sin he had committed in his life, stepped into an aisle. He was trembling under conviction and lifted a hand to get Peter's attention. The crowd turned to look at this respected elder from the town. Peter, having never given an altar call before, didn't know if calling on this man to speak was in order or not. But the little man could not hold it in any longer. "Well preacher, tell us what to do. I recognize my sin. I am ashamed that I was one of the reasons the Messiah was crucified. I don't have much time left on this earth and I want to make things right with God. Tell me preacher, what must I do?"

"Then Peter said unto them, Repent, and be baptized every one of you in the name of Jesus Christ for the remission of sins, and ye shall receive the gift of the Holy Ghost. For the promise is unto you, and to your children, and to all that are afar off, even as many as the Lord our God shall call. And with many other words did he testify and exhort, saying, Save yourselves from this untoward generation. Then they that gladly received his word were baptized: and the same day there were added unto them about three thousand souls" (Acts 2:38-41).

Peter's incredibly successful message on the day of Pentecost should inspire every one of us to resolve to preach the gospel. Place Jesus at the center of every message. Let the reality of the Cross permeate every sermon. And when conviction falls, the hearers will respond in faith and obey the gospel.

"So shall my word be that goes out from my mouth; it shall not return to me empty, but it shall accomplish that which I purpose, and shall succeed in the thing for which I sent it" (Isaiah 55:11, ESV).

When you preach, you are doing something that is guaranteed to succeed. We can be certain that the preached Word of God will succeed in its purposes of edification and evangelism.

We should preach with confidence. God's Word will produce the results promised in His Word.

What is the most important part of the sermon?

The most important part of the sermon is knowing what you want the sermon to do to the people to whom you are preaching. You must know what you want the sermon to accomplish. It is not the beginning of it, the middle of it, or the ending of it. In my mind, the sermon is not divided up into parts. When you teach preaching, yes it has parts. But the whole thing is a message. You are moving people from point A to point B. If you are not intending to move people from A to B with this sermon then you are only giving a speech. A sermon, a message is supposed to move people. If you don't know what you want people to believe when you are finished, then you are not going to preach it with passion.

The most important part of the sermon is the purpose of the sermon. Why should I even take the breath and time to say this stuff? If I don't know that, then I will lose the anointing and the passion—I will lose it all. Before I preach a message I ask myself, "Why are you preaching this sermon?" If I don't know this, then all that is important is for me to get through my set of notes. But if I know what I want people to believe when I finish, then the notes are just a track to run on and I can preach with passion. God will be able to drop those things I couldn't think of in my head, because the goal is not getting through my notes but it is to move people. That's the most important part of the sermon. Where do you want these people to be moved to by the time you get through with the message?

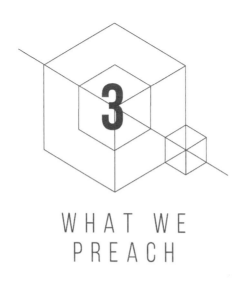

WHAT WE
PREACH

If a person hungering for God comes into your church, "it is because he wants to know what Christians believe and what God has to say. Can you imagine the disappointment you might feel if, having overcome the overwhelming inertia and having actually shown up in church, you didn't hear anything different from what you might have heard on Oprah? You didn't have to get off the couch for that. When seekers come to church, somewhere inside they are hoping that they might hear from God."[10]

No doubt many of us have been exposed to various types of public speaking genres. Lecture series frequently appear on university campuses. Most high schools have debate clubs where students learn persuasive speaking. Law schools teach their students to craft arguments around the case evidence and legal rules. World leaders deliver speeches to give their countries and the rest of the world hope, vision, and assurance they are doing what is best for the people.

Preaching must be persuasive, just like the debate teams are taught. Preaching, at times will contain arguments in an effort to convince the jury—those sitting along the sidelines—they need to make a certain decision. Preaching should give hope, articulate vision, and give the congregation assurance, just like the world leaders aim to do. But preaching cannot become any of these alone. Preaching must declare the Bible. All true preaching is biblical.

Unless you declare the Bible, there will be no conviction. It is conviction that spawns lasting change. It is conviction that causes a sinner to cry out to a God who can save them. No matter how well you craft your words, your sentences, or your arguments, you cannot convict anyone. Conviction is a work of the Spirit born out of the Word of God.

Those who pride themselves on harsh preaching may be surprised to learn that sometimes such messages are not biblical because they are motivated by the wrath of the speaker rather than the grace and power of God. Perhaps they can produce a feeling of guilt in those who are listening, but a feeling of guilt alone is not conviction. No preacher has the ability to bring true conviction on his or her audience. We do not preach conviction under our own power or by our own ability. Conviction is not something we conjure up by our sheer talent at wielding the right words or telling a moving story from our illustration files. The Word alone has the power to bring conviction.

In the act of convicting, the Holy Spirit takes on several roles. The Spirit exposes sin like an attorney. It reproves the sinner like a judge. However, a lifeline of mercy is held out to the sinner. The sinner is not simply convicted and sentenced to hell. The sinner feels the conviction of his or her sin and is convinced of the need for a Savior. It matters not how steeped in sin someone may be. It matters not how far away from God they have travelled. The Word will convict and show those who are hungry the way back to God.

Around sixteen years of age, King Josiah began to "seek the God of his father David." (See II Chronicles 34:3, NIV.) This hunger for God led to some degree of reform in Judah. He tore down idols, smashed to pieces the altars of Baal, and began a nationwide purging that was a catalyst for revival.

All of this came from a deeply rooted desire to please God and get back to the old paths.

But it wasn't until God's Word was found that true conviction completely changed the king's heart.

> *While they were bringing out the money that had been taken into the temple of the Lord, Hilkiah the priest found the Book of the Law of the Lord that had been given through Moses. Hilkiah said to Shaphan the secretary, "I have found the Book of the Law in the temple of the Lord." He gave it to Shaphan. Then Shaphan took the book to the king and reported to him: "Your officials are doing everything that has been committed to them. They have paid out the money that was in the temple of the Lord and have entrusted it to the supervisors and workers." Then Shaphan the secretary informed the king, "Hilkiah the priest has given me a book." And Shaphan read from it in the presence of the king. When the king heard the words of the Law, he tore his robes. He gave these orders to Hilkiah, Ahikam son of Shaphan, Abdon son of Micah, Shaphan the secretary and Asaiah the king's attendant: "Go and inquire of the Lord for me and for the remnant in Israel and Judah about what is written in this book that has been found. Great is the Lord's anger that is poured out on us because those who have gone before us have not kept the word of the Lord, they have not acted in accordance with all that is written in this book"* (II Chronicles 34:14-21, NIV).

Everyone has the ability, to some degree, to recognize right and wrong. It may be from lessons they were taught by their parents or grandparents. It may simply be the conscience God has given each of us. King Josiah made his initial reforms in Judah because of conscience and because of what he had learned from his past. But when the Word of God was read to him, he realized the Lord was angry and that Judah had not "acted in accordance with all that is written in this book" (II Chronicles 34:21, NIV).

The congregation needs to be invited to look at themselves in the mirror of the Word through biblical preaching. They need to recognize their sin and see it as God sees it. People can more easily reconcile their wrong-doing if they feel some other human is trying to judge them. But if they see their sin through the lens of God's Word, they are arguing with God when they choose to defend their ways.

Let the Word of God convict. Be honest with yourself as you prepare each sermon. Is there too much human argument and influence? Am I building my case based on God's Word or am I relying on other means of convincing my audience? As a preacher, hopefully you learn, develop, and improve in the practice of preaching. But no matter how much you learn, develop, and improve, you must never give the Word of God mere sporadic cameo appearances in the messages you preach.

Once you get away from the Word, the message loses power. Stories, illustrations, clever thoughts, quotes, and examples from life all help impact the overall theme and secure the interest of the audience. But the overall theme must be rooted in Scripture. Preaching is not preaching unless the Word of God is at the heart of the message.

"The foundational basis for anyone's relationship with God is that they hear His Word and respond to it."[11]

We have to make sure new believers start off on the right foot. Events are wonderful ways to attract new people, but people will not last until they are grounded in the Word. The same is true for Christians who should be more committed than they are. If their commitment is only based upon their involvement in ministry or any other avenue of busyness in the church, the chances are they will not last the test of time.

Yes, we need to involve people in the life of the church as soon as we can, but we cannot count on their involvement being the glue that holds their spiritual life together. Their relationship with God must be rooted and grounded in His Word.

I find nowhere in Scripture that tells me Adam and Eve actually saw God. We really don't know if He appeared to them when He walked with them in the cool of the day. But they did hear God. It was God's voice—God's very words— upon which their relationship with Him was built. We do not know how many conversations they had with God before they each gave in to the temptation offered them by the serpent, but we understand that it was through these conversations they came to know God.

It was God's very Word that was questioned by the serpent when he enticed Eve: "Hath God said?" (Genesis 3:1). The enemy knows the power of God's Word. His most basic attack on mankind is in the realm of what God has said. Thus, today as never before, we see an attack on preaching and the authority of declaring God's Word. If the enemy can undermine either the messenger or the message, he can defeat the very thing that has the power to draw men and women to the Lord: God's Word.

The enemy is not afraid of your human arguments. He is not afraid of how eloquent you can become. He is not afraid of how creative your object lessons are. He is not afraid of the emotion you show when you preach. The enemy understands those kinds of speeches are a dime a dozen. What he is afraid of is someone who is convinced of God's Word, has experienced its power in their own lives, and knows how to deliver it so that it cuts deep to the heart. "For the word of God is quick, and powerful, and sharper than any two-edged sword, piercing even to the dividing asunder of soul and spirit, and of the joints and marrow, and is a discerner of the thoughts and intents of the heart" (Hebrews 4:12).

Abraham did not have a relationship with the one true God until Genesis 12:1: "Now the Lord had said unto Abram." His entire walk of faith can be traced back to that moment—

when God spoke to him. When Abraham had nothing else to go on, He stood on God's promise. When others didn't believe him and doubted the direction he was headed, He stood on God's Word.

It appears fifteen to twenty years passed between God speaking to Abram about leaving Ur and then God speaking to him again after their fifteen-year hiatus in Haran. God's Word has the power to keep you. When you get a hold of a word from God, nothing can convince you to let go of that word. Somehow in our preaching, we must pray people get a hold of a word from God. That cannot happen if God's Word is not being proclaimed. Give your congregation something to hold onto. Give them the Word above anything else.

We must not simply hear the Word, we must apply what we hear to our lives.

"Take to heart all the words by which I am warning you today, that you may command them to your children, that they may be careful to do all the words of this law. For it is no empty word for you, but your very life" (Deuteronomy 32:46-47, ESV).

The Word of God is our very life. The Word of God that sustains us and leads us must be passed on to the next generation. What legacy are we passing on as preachers to the next generation? Are we passing on "How to Become a Better Leader" based on the writings of the latest leadership guru? Or instead: "Keep this Book of the Law always on your lips; meditate on it day and night, so that you may be careful to do everything written in it. Then you will be prosperous and successful" (Joshua 1:8, NIV). Preach the Word. Preach God-help, not self-help.

We are responsible for raising a generation of churchgoers who are not biblically illiterate. We can only do so much in the fifty-two Sundays we are given each year. But our limited opportunities make it even more important that we not waste any moment we are given to preach the Word.

No wonder the majority of preaching schools around the world teach their students that expository preaching is the only way to preach. Expository preaching is taking a passage—sometimes a few verses, sometimes an entire chapter—and preaching the intended meaning of that passage. In other words, the author's intended meaning of those verses and his main idea of that passage becomes the main idea of your message. Expository preaching therefore is beneficial in educating your congregation on the true meaning of biblical passages. We can't simply carve up books and chapters by pulling one verse out, preaching on it alone, and forgetting that it was a part of a larger message being communicated by the author.

If we preach from a single verse and ignore the context of that verse, we fail to preach the author's intended message. Our congregations end up viewing Scripture as a fractured group of individual verses instead of one, large, overarching narrative. We even teach them to read the Bible this way. Pick one chapter from this book, one chapter from that, and maybe a psalm or proverb. Most of our saints don't know that the original writers didn't write in chapter and verse format. They don't realize the entire book of Ephesians should be viewed as one single manuscript. They never get the full message.

More often than not, preaching in Pentecostal circles is topical. We try to be true to the text—hoping we don't take the verse out of context—but instead of preaching the meaning of a passage, we become enamored by a word or phrase and launch our message from there. This is not wrong, and sometimes can be very effective. However, we often fail to be well-rounded and systematic. We end up not preaching the whole counsel of God because of a select few candy-stick subjects we tend to go back to time and time again.

There are subjects we should revisit from time to time. But when some truths are neglected due to the time we spend on other truths, we build imbalanced churches. Therefore we should plan and systematically choose preaching topics. Of course, we should always make room for those moments when the Lord says, "Preach this." But in the meantime, until you hear that direct command, just preach through the Word.

As a side note, we can also fall into a rut of choosing our topic before we choose a Bible passage. We get a cool thought from a website, a magazine, a book, or even a conversation with a friend, and then we look for a verse to back up our thought. If that is happening more often than you getting a thought from Scripture, then it might be a good time to ask yourself, "What kind of diet am I feeding my church"?

The Power of Words

Carefully choose your words when preparing your sermon and preaching. However, keep in mind our words cannot do what God's Word can do. We will use our words when we preach, but unless our words are communicating God's Word, our preaching is in vain!

There is power and authority in the preached Word of God. We should make sure that "the proclamation of God's Word" is "the central component of our ministry. When competing priorities and competing philosophies tempt us sorely to displace the preaching of the Word from the center, the valley of the dry bones . . . ought to remind us that true spiritual-life-giving power is found in God's Word. That is how our God, in His wisdom, has determined to give life to His people."[12]

Ezekiel only saw one clear option when he was set before the valley of dry bones. God was going to have to do the work. When asked by God, "can these bones live?" Ezekiel responded, "Lord, only You know." (See Ezekiel 37:3.)

If God was truly asking Ezekiel to figure out a way to resurrect this dead army, the prophet knew this was not something humanly possible. He probably knew very little about human anatomy. Even with present-day medical advancements, piecing together dead bones is for museums, not hospitals. So if anything miraculous was going to happen, God was going to have to do the work. This was the only option Ezekiel could see.

Then God spoke again. "Prophesy to these bones and say to them, 'Dry bones, hear the word of the LORD!'" (Ezekiel 37:4, NIV). Preach to the bones? What good will that do? I don't know how to tell them to come alive! I don't know how to tell bones and flesh to come back together. How many of us feel the same way when we stand before our congregations, viewing the carnage of broken homes, broken lives, and shattered hopes? What good will it do if I tell them it will all be all right?

Exactly. In and of your own ability, you can't. Your own clever words, thoughts, and stories can't do anything of lasting consequence for them. But God didn't tell Ezekiel to come up with some creative message to really wow the dead audience. God said to speak to them the words He would give him. "Dry bones, hear the word of the LORD!" It is not your word. It is His Word. Your words will fall way short. His Word will resurrect the dead.

Some people will look at preaching as just another option on a list of many options for people to learn about God and His Word. And other ways are much more entertaining and less formal and "preachy." They would rather read a good book, watch some video clips online, listen to some Christian talk show by either radio or podcast, or just have a nice, non-judgmental conversation with another Christian.

But if preaching "really is the proclamation of God's life-giving, ex nihilo creating Word, then the stakes are raised considerably, and it's no longer a matter of preference whether we do it or not. It's literally a matter of life and death. The Bible presents the act of preaching as having just that sort of power and authority. It is the preached Word, it seems, which the Holy Spirit uses in a unique way to give life and ignite faith in a person's soul."[13]

Why do we feel we need to help the Word? Why do we feel we have to be cute and clever when preaching, so that we mask the Word of God behind our humor or slick presentation? Are we afraid the Word doesn't have the power it claims to have? I am by no means postulating we forgo any kind of creativity when it comes to preaching, but that we ask ourselves how much we really trust the Word.

"Too many churches today have preachers looking to culture around them, not simply for the most effective methods of communicating their message but for the most effective message to be preached."[14]

Are we afraid the Word will be boring to our hearers? Well, is it boring to you? If so, immerse yourself in the Word. Pray over your heart. Rearrange your schedule, find some alone time, and meditate on God's Word. Let the Word become a priority in your life. Start the day with the Word. End the day with the Word. If we want to be preachers who please God, we must make God's Word a priority in our lives.

I have one single picture in my mind when I think of my grandmother McClintock. She suffered with rheumatoid arthritis for decades. I didn't know her when she wasn't sick. The last several years of her life she was confined to her home. Grandpa would carry her to the couch every morning and then to the bed every evening. But that isn't the picture in my mind. While I do think of that when I think of her, the one picture I cannot help but see in my head when I think of her, is her feeble frame huddled on the couch, knees together, with her Bible open on her lap. She loved the Word of God.

When you talked with her, the Word came out of her mouth. When you spent time with her, you knew she had been spending time in the Word. The Word became the very breath she breathed. It truly was her daily manna. It was not boring. It was life.

If you are passionate about the Word of God, that passion will permeate the entire sermon. I have heard preachers who are captivating when they are reading their text. The words flow from their lips as if they are Peter, Paul, or John, dictating their thoughts to a scribe.

When you have quoted Scripture in a sermon—verses that have meant so much to you during your lifetime—did you speak it differently than a passage you read, but had not become very familiar with? Take time to internalize as much of the Word as you can before you preach it. Not everything has to be memorized, but it should be internalized.

I think sometimes we forget the inherent power residing in the Word of God. We seek long and hard for clever thoughts no one has ever thought of before, hoping our creativity captivates them and their lives are forever changed. Trust in the Word. Instead of making it harder than it really is, just preach the Word.

How do you stay motivated to preach on a regular basis even when you are tired, stressed, or just plain lacking the "want to"?

Everybody has to have two streams and not one. Psalm 1:3 says, "he shall be like a tree planted by the rivers of water, that bringeth forth his fruit in his season; his leaf also shall not wither; and whatsoever he doeth shall prosper." The reason why that tree is always producing fruit is because it has roots way down in the soil. There is a hidden supply of water because it is by the riverbed. The river may dry up but the root structure is way down in the soil and it's tapping into water the surface doesn't see. Every preacher has to have his personal relationship with God. He has to have things God speaks to him that are not for sermons.

I had a young preacher talk to me about being mentored this week. One of the things he said as he got honest with me was, "Honestly, I just study the Bible to get sermons. I don't really know the Word of God for myself. And I don't even know how to hear the voice of God for myself." And that is why he is not a full-time preacher right now. That's why he's working a job and he just preaches out occasionally. Because he has not understood that being a preacher is not just creating sermons. There has to be a supply. There has to be depth. I cannot take you to a place I've never been myself. So I could preach to you about Canaan land, but if I'm not there myself, then it's just a nice idea for all of us. It's like someone preaching about the Holy Ghost that has never received it. You can't really preach about it. You can say, "Well, I believe it's out there and you can have it. I don't have it yet." You have to have your own personal time with God, where you're drinking from that well.

Then there's that second stream which is that river you are by: that stream of the anointing, revelation, and purpose. As long as you're in that and you flow in that, you'll always have things to say.

God showed me this early on in my ministry. He told me, "Stop worrying. The prophets of old never worried about where to preach, they only worried about what to preach." He said, "If you are hearing My voice, and you are finding out what I want to say, I will always have a place for you to say it." So I became a passionate pursuer of the voice of God. "God, what are You saying to the church right now?" "He that has an ear to hear. . ." That's what I want to know. This is what keeps me motivated. This is what keeps me alive. What keeps me functioning is that I'm hearing from God. As long as I am hearing from God and I have a personal stream of God speaking to me, I'll always have a stream for everybody else. But if I am not hearing God for myself, my river is going to run dry and my branch is going to wither.

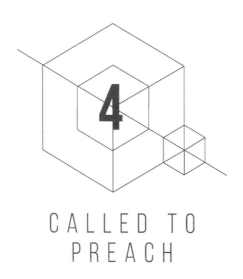

CALLED TO
PREACH

All believers who have fully submitted to God and obeyed the gospel have the ability to recognize the calling placed upon their lives. Paul told the Ephesian congregation to "walk worthy of the vocation wherewith ye are called" (Ephesians 4:1). To "live a life worthy of the calling you have received" (Ephesians 4:1, NIV).

Paul assumed all the Ephesian believers had a calling on their life. The statement is a general admonition because each of these individuals will end up living out their calling in different ways. But for some, and quite possibly you, the calling will be lived out through the avenue of preaching.

I believe many are self-called. In other words, to many, the preaching ministry is just a profession and not a Divine Calling. Some are influenced to get into the preaching ministry because of someone else they admire or envy. Some may even think, "I want to be the guy behind the pulpit who gets all the attention and gets to tell everybody what he thinks."

However, it is of utmost importance for each man and woman who is considering the calling of a preacher to understand the call of God to the ministry of the Word is a call sovereignly exercised by the Holy Spirit. Those whom God has called to preach are set apart specifically for that purpose. It is not wise to launch into the practice of preaching if you are not convinced the Holy Ghost has called you to do so.

The Preacher's Calling

Here are some things to consider as you contemplate your calling to preach the Word of God.

First of all, God is not going to call anyone who does not have the capability to hear Him call. In other words, one must be a genuine believer, because only genuine believers can hear His call to preach. Most everyone in the church fits this criterion, but truly this is not the only condition for this call.

"To be called by God into the preaching ministry, one must have the capacity to hear Him call (only believers); one must actually hear Him call (in tune with God); and one must answer or obey the call (surrender to fulfill the call of God and actually engage in a preaching ministry).

It is more than a 'want to.' It is a 'have to.' It is alright to want to preach but the Divine Call gives you a sense that you have to preach as well. If you don't have that urgency, it is very possible you are not called to preach—at least not by God. In fact, as someone appropriately said, 'If you are in tune with God and you can do anything else besides the preaching ministry, then do it. He's not calling or you would hear Him loud and clear.'"[15]

I have met young men and young women who have wanted to preach. Their hearts seemed to be right. They were good people. They loved God and wanted to work in His kingdom more than anything. However, their fascination with preaching confused them. Since they knew preaching was so important, and they wanted to do what was important, they felt compelled to pursue a preaching ministry. Perhaps I am oversimplifying things. But I say it in this way because, I feel the majority of those who pursue preaching, even when they are not called to preach, have hearts that desire to please God.

Maybe this is a good time to examine your motives. Why do you want to preach? Are you convinced of the calling? Are you not quite sure, but you know you want to do something for God? Are you feeling pressure from those around you to preach?

For many reading this book, this issue has already been settled. Perhaps you have already been serving in the preaching ministry for a while now. The truth is, you will encounter those in your ministry who are struggling with this as they seek the will of God for their life.

I remember as a young boy attending New Life Christian School in Bridgeton, Missouri. During my time there, I began sensing a call of God on my life. In the seventh and eighth grades, I worked in the kitchen a couple days a week with Sister Adams.

When I would walk down the hall toward the cafeteria and kitchen, I could hear the preacher on the radio get louder and louder. Turning to walk into the kitchen, I saw Sister Adams beginning to prepare lunch, listening to the voice of R. W. Schambach over the radio waves. And I can remember it like it was yesterday. Sister Adams would stop what she was doing, look me in the eyes and say, "There's my little preacher."

I treasure that memory, and I am grateful for her and others who would say things like that out of concern for my future. However, even the most encouraging voices can contribute to confusion when a young man or woman is trying to figure out what all this desire and hunger inside really means. Am I called to preach or am I just enjoying all the nice things people are saying?

Even parents can push their kids to head in directions that may not be ordained by God. We all understand the fine line some parents try to walk when pushing their kids to do something they wish they would have done when they were younger. We call this "living vicariously" through someone else. Parents do not intend to steer children in the wrong direction, but will sometimes feel like they are doing the right thing and are "looking out for" their children.

Parents need to be careful when it comes to pushing their children into a career or calling, especially when it comes to the role of a preacher. Only God calls individuals to preach the gospel. Even with their grand intentions, parents or other well-meaning family members can end up contributing more confusion to the already confusing pursuit of figuring out one's life calling.

Merrill F. Unger says, "There are many ways in which the call may come—directly or indirectly, through circumstances. But come it must! Preaching God's Word is important work. God does the selecting, the calling and the empowering for this momentous task. Laymen may preach and teach the Bible and do it well. But when God calls a man to give his full time to the ministry of the Word, that man ought to know he is divinely called and commissioned for this sacred occupation. Moreover, God intends that he should know and graciously extends His call, so that no preacher ought to be without this divine assurance."[16]

> A preacher is not a Christian who decides to preach, he does not just decide to do it; he does not even decide to take up preaching as a calling . . . This picture of the type of life lived by the minister has often appealed to young men, and there have been many who have gone into the ministry in that way. I need scarcely say that this is entirely wrong and quite foreign to the picture one gets in the Scriptures, and also as one reads the lives of the great preachers throughout the centuries. The answer to that false view is that preaching is never something that a man decides to do. What happens rather is that he becomes conscious of a "call."[17]

This whole idea of understanding the call to preach is not easy. All ministers have struggled with it. Authority to do the work of God must come from God. How can one speak in the name of another without having been commissioned to do so?

The Jews marveled at Jesus "because he spoke as one having authority, and not as the scribes" (Matthew 7:29). Jesus revealed the source of His authority when he read these words from the scroll in the temple:

"The Spirit of the Lord is upon me, because he hath anointed me to preach the gospel to the poor; he hath sent me to heal the brokenhearted, to preach deliverance to the captives, and recovering of sight to the blind, to set at liberty them that are bruised, To preach the acceptable year of the Lord" (Luke 4:18-19).

This anointed authority to preach must not be taken lightly. "The non-commissioned preacher not only brings upon himself the scorn of men, but subjects himself to the judgment of a despised and rejected God."[18]

The Old Testament warns of the dire consequences of speaking a word God has not sent. "The prophet who speaks a word presumptuously in My name which I have not commanded him to speak, or which he speaks in the name of other gods, that prophet shall die" (Deuteronomy 18:20, NASB).

Therefore you must approach preaching with reverence. As you seek to understand the presence or absence of a divine call of God to preach, begin preparing your heart, mind, and body for an answer. Of course, this advice is good for all believers, not just those wrestling with a call to preach.

1. Make sure your body has become a living and sanctified sacrifice unto the Lord. (See Romans 12:1-2.)
2. Make sure there is no conscious sin dulling your spiritual ear and spiritual sight. (See Ephesians 1:18-19.)
3. Make sure you are willing to go and to be used anywhere. (See John 7:17.)
4. Form the habit of daily prayer, Bible study, and private meditations before the Lord. (See Joshua 1:8; Psalms 77:12; 119:15, 25, 45.)

5. Study carefully the Word of God. Become saturated with the Word of God. (See Psalms 119:11, 104-105)
6. Study carefully the great spiritual needs of our day and prepare to meet them. (See John 4:35.)
7. Pray regularly and earnestly that God will make His will and call definite for you. (See Psalms 25:4; 27:11; 143:8.)[19]

Though realizing the call of God to preach can become confusing for some, it is important to understand the practical ways in which God will speak to the individual about his or her calling. God does not have intentions to confuse the sincere seeker, but wants to make His calling sure for the individual.

First of all, one way in which God speaks to individuals about a call to preach is through others in their lives. Very often someone else will recognize a genuine call to preach on your life. This can be a confusing proposition when parents and other well-meaning family members believe you are called to preach; however, you may feel more confident when others, such as a pastor, elder minister, or God-directed layperson recognize something resting upon your life. In fact, this is important in the process. Those in authority, under whom you have placed yourself, will often see something in you before you do. Do not be surprised when you talk to your pastor about a call to preach if he speaks confidently to you about the call he has already recognized upon your life.

God will also, at times, confirm His call for you to preach through the reading of His Word. As you meditate upon the Scriptures, oftentimes that Word will become in you a fire to which you feel you must deliver to others, telling them of God's work and plan for their lives. As a preacher you will be spending a lot of time in God's Word. So as you seek His will, spend extended periods of time reading and meditating on His Word. In fact, since it is the Word of God you will be preaching, becoming familiar with it is of utmost importance. The prophet Ezekiel recorded several times in which "the Word of the LORD came to me" (See Ezekiel 29:17; 30:20; 31:1;

32:1, 17). As a preacher, the Word of the Lord will come to you, and it is the Word of the Lord that you will preach.

For some, God extends His call through difficult life circumstances and situations. Consider the fact that Isaiah received his call in the year of King Uzziah's death. The passing of this good king created uncertainty in the kingdom, but God had a plan to raise up Isaiah to help the next king.

Some scholars argue that Isaiah's vision in chapter 6 was not when the prophet received his initial calling to the ministry, but rather an introduction into a more specific calling and purpose. Whatever the case, we can still recognize the crisis the nation (including Isaiah) was experiencing and how that influenced the willingness of Isaiah to respond to God's call: "Here I am. Lord, send me."

In addition, the call of God to preach will often be confirmed through sound, logical thinking. Of course, there are numerous instances in Scripture where it appeared God did things completely out of the ordinary or at least in a way the mind of man had not before considered. However, that is not the case in every situation. In fact, it is God who created each of us with the ability to think soundly, logically, and with common sense.

Paul told Timothy that God has given us all a "sound mind." (See II Timothy 1:7.) "Sound mind" literally refers to self-discipline in that verse, but the understanding is the same. Through sound, disciplined thinking in our minds, God will reveal His call. To some, the call of God will not make sense at first. But God's call always makes sense when weighed in accordance with God's plan and purpose for you and your life.

For you to be successful in your call to preach, you must become genuinely persuaded of the call of God. This strong persuasion will be evident in several ways. First of all, there needs to be a deep sense of humility and personal inadequacy when it comes to fulfilling this calling. This does not mean that you walk around talking negatively to yourself, feeling insignificant and shameful because you know you are unworthy. Instead, it should be an attitude of gratefulness and one of indebtedness. Because God has called you, you feel blessed and honored He would choose you to carry on His work.

Next to that is acquiring the confidence you need to become convinced that you can do the job, with God's help. Realize you have the ability to do what God is calling you to do if you will simply prepare yourself through consecration of your heart and spirit, and through the study of God's Word.

"Study to shew thyself approved unto God, a workman that needeth not to be ashamed, rightly dividing the word of truth" (II Timothy 2:15).

Not only must you recognize your ability to answer the call and succeed, but you also must be willing to do whatever it takes to secure that ability. You must be willing to prepare well. Laziness will catch up to you.

There is a phrase used by entrepreneurs and athletes alike: "going all in." What is meant by these three words? When a woman starts a new business or an athlete is train- ing for gold, these words simply mean they are going to do everything they can to achieve their goals . . . nothing will stand in their way. To go all in, means that every ounce of energy, every thought, and every moment will be spent eyeing the goal, planning the next move, and preparing for nothing but success.

Those who are called to preach must "go all in." They must be committed and completely yielded to the Lord and the calling to which they have been set apart. In fact, the reality is, only those who are completely committed will find themselves completely satisfied with the work God does through them.

Andre M. Rogers, professor of pastoral ministries at Columbia International University, suggests five questions the man or woman who feels a call to preach should ask them- selves:[20]

1. "Do I meet the qualifications of a preacher as set forth in the Word of God? (See I Timothy 3:1-7; Titus 1:5-9.)"
2. "Do I have the witness of the Spirit in my heart that God has called me? In Nehemiah Chapter 1 we discover that the minister has to receive a burden from God. Remain open to how God will use the Spirit to direct you."
3. "Has the gift of preaching become evident in my life and service? If you have the gift of preaching there is an internal enjoyment and a spiritual hunger to preach. Your passion and desire will be to preach God's Word."
4. "Has my church recognized and confirmed my preaching gifts?"
5. "Has God used my preaching gift to the salvation of souls and the building up of the church? If no one is being changed or challenged then preaching may not be for you!"

Finally, if you recognize what feels like a genuine call to preach on your life, here are five things you must do:[21]

First of all, announce your call. Make the calling known to those you love and those who will be the most supportive. Also, you need to announce your call to your pastor and those in authority in your life. Some seminaries actually require a vote from the local church, approving of the candidate, thus confirming their calling before they are allowed to even be considered for acceptance into the seminary program.

Second, and this may sound like a given, but continue being a good Christian. Recognizing a call on your life to preach does not give permission to begin living any differently than you had been as a committed disciple of Jesus Christ. In fact, you may need to ramp up your commitment level and your dedication to your personal spiritual disciplines.

Third, don't stop exercising your spiritual gifts. Continue serving under your pastor in your local church congregation. There are more spiritual gifts that need to be exercised in the church besides the gift of prophecy (preaching). Serve the church well. Serve the leadership of the church well. Learn as much as you can under the direction of your pastor, and God will honor you.

Fourth, pray about how you should train to do the ministry God has called you to do. Whether you pursue formal education, intern under a spiritual leader, or participate in some combination of the two, the truth is, you need training. If you launch into anything (let alone the ministry of preaching) without proper training and education, your path to success will be hindered. The proper training will help you identify obstacles and opportunities you may have never seen coming without instruction.

Finally, let God lead you into your lifelong ministry calling. Remember God is the One who called you. And if He called you, He will order and direct your steps.

Who has made the biggest impact on you as a preacher?

In his day, without a doubt, my pastor George L. Glass, Sr. was the greatest pulpit preacher in the UPC. He was a dynamic pastor and preacher. Above all of his abilities, the man was a Christian. We saw his life: prayer life, study life. We saw him walk through some of the darkest valleys a man could ever walk through. But he was never anything but a Christian through it all. That taught me so much.

Howard Goss used to tell us, "First I am a Christian, second I am a preacher, and thirdly I am an official. If being an official ever interferes with me being a preacher, I will quit being an official. If being a preacher ever interferes with me being a Christian, I will quit being a preacher. Because I want to end up, not an official, not a preacher, but a Christian." There's not going to be any preachers in Heaven, only worshipers. You won't need any preachers up there. You better emphasize on earth what you are going to do the longest in eternity.

I travelled a lot with A. T. Morgan (the second general superintendent of the UPCI) who was one of my mentors. I spent days and hours traveling with Oliver Fauss. These men were great mentors and always had the highest integrity and principles. The ministry is a character profession. If you lose your character, you lose everything. A brain surgeon can sleep with a different woman every night and still successfully operate on my brain. But the ministry is a character profession. Men and women of character impress me as much or more than ability. What you are out of the pulpit contributes to more of your ministry that what you are in the pulpit.

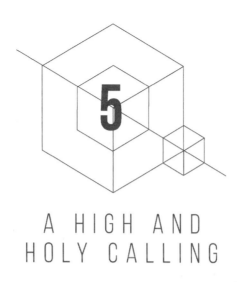

A HIGH AND
HOLY CALLING

INTERVIEW
WITH
TERRY PUGH

Below are comments taken from an interview with Terry Pugh, pastor of First United Pentecostal Church (Odessa, Texas), on the topic of the high calling of the preacher:

Do you feel there is a disconnect today between the preacher (his calling) and the way he lives (his lifestyle)?

I would eliminate the word "today." It seems to be the responsibility of every generation to explain that the younger generation is not as good as the present generation. Biblically, there was Demas, who was with the apostle Paul. He was a man who evidently had a call of God on his life. He was an intern, a student of the man who wrote most of the New Testament. He was a part of the Book of Acts church. But somewhere in that process he lost sight of the value of this life of preaching, this calling of preaching . . . he lost it.

Paul admitted to this struggle of integrity. In Romans he admitted, "When I want to do good, I end up doing evil." Paul let us know that it is always a struggle. Integrity doesn't come naturally. The flesh comes naturally. He mentioned the works of the flesh; things that no one has to work at. Those come naturally. But integrity is something for which we must strive. To live Christ-like is something that is to be practiced every day.

That is why I think I would eliminate the word "today." Yes, there is a disconnect today. There was a disconnect with the greatest generation. We put them on a pedestal. There were great men who founded the United Pentecostal Church. But there were also men in that generation who fell. They weren't all perfect just because they were a part of the greatest generation. They had their struggles. They had their flaws just like we have our flaws. So it's not just today. Every generation struggles with integrity, struggles with being a Christian one hundred percent through and through.

How important is the life of the preacher in connection with their calling?

I'm reminded of Paul saying, "I've got to keep my body under subjection." All of us have witnessed individuals who were great preachers—they could preach. But eventually it was discovered that they were short on character. It may take years. But poor character will eventually reduce the influence, caliber, and calling of a preacher. The life of a preacher cannot be separated from their calling and preaching. You see it happen in the religious world and specifically in our organization. Men compartmentalize: "I'm a preacher" and "I'm a man." But you can't do that and be all God wants you to be. You must understand that "I am not like every other man."

The preacher's life is everything. And that is a pretty big word. You cannot truly separate a preacher's life from their calling. Once you are called, you are something different. You are something special. You have been handpicked by God. You have been chosen by God Almighty. It comes down to: You are called by God. . . . And for Him to call me who He knows is made out of dust, who He knows is imperfect and flawed, to be involved in what He determined is the most important thing He is doing on the planet. That is awesome! And I can't lose sight of that.

If I lose sight of that, then I will try to blend in with the people of the church or with people in society. Now I don't want anyone to put me on a pedestal, nor do I want to think of myself on a pedestal, but God has called me to be a preacher. And because God has called me to be a preacher, I must live in a way that pleases the One who has called me.

Second Timothy 2:4 says, "No soldier gets entangled in civilian pursuits, since his aim is to please the one who enlisted him" (ESV). That's the way we must be as preachers. We must live in a way that is pleasing to the One Who has called us into this great calling.

How important is preaching today in the twenty-first century?

Preaching is the highest calling. It is the most important thing that anybody can do. It has been said that during Abraham Lincoln's presidency, a preacher applied for one of his open cabinet positions. Lincoln told the preacher that taking this position would mean the preacher would have to stoop down from his high calling.

Romans 10:13-14 says, "For whosoever shall call upon the name of the Lord shall be saved. How then shall they call on Him in whom they have not believed? And how shall they believe in Him of Whom they have not heard? And how shall they hear without a preacher?" We are talking about people's salvation. Salvation is a Heaven or Hell issue. This is not something we can do as a hobby. Nobody can be saved unless they believe they can be saved and know they can be saved. How can they believe unless they hear? And they cannot hear without a preacher.

According to Paul, the preacher is the key to salvation for every human being on the planet. Without a preacher, the odds of anybody in the world being saved are about zip. We place a lot of value on Bible study teachers, and they are valuable. But the bottom line is: if somebody is not preaching, then salvation is not going to happen. In addition, it takes a preacher to maintain that salvation in their lives. . .

Paul said in I Corinthians 1:17, "Christ sent me not to baptize, but to preach the gospel." We make a big deal about church growth, a crowd, and how many we baptized. The emphasis should not be so much the numbers, but did you preach the truth? He didn't call me just to baptize a bunch of people; He called me to preach the Gospel. And Paul goes on to say, "And it pleased God by the foolishness of preaching to save them that believe." There we go again: if anybody is going to be saved, it will be done through preaching. You can't get away from the value of preaching.

What is the one thing you would tell an audience of young preachers who want to make a difference and preach the Gospel?

I would wrap it up in this statement: "God Called You." Then I would emphasize each of those words. God. Called. You.

God.

Not your pastor, your mother, nor your friends; God called you. You can't afford to take preaching lightly. You can't take your life casually. When I keep reminding myself that "I am called by God," dimension and weight are added to my life. I am called by God. So when I get ready to quit, when I get discouraged, I come back to the fact "I don't have a right to quit or get discouraged. I am called by Almighty God." Out of seven billion people in the planet, God chose me. The One who knows all things; the One who knows the happenings of the year 2020 as much as He knows 1831. That God, the one who can speak and create stars, trees, and flowers. That God chose me and invited me to be a part of what He is doing in the world. God called me. The emphasis is on that. I'm not just a preacher. I am a God-called preacher.

The second is "Called." I am called, selected, and chosen. I can never forget that I am selected and anointed by God. God did this. It is not my idea. I wanted to own a business, but God selected me to do something more important with my life. Knowing the fact that I have been called by God is enough to affect the choices I make and the way I live. I am not just any man. I am an anointed, called man. It is a special calling. I cannot take it lightly or treat it casually. A preacher should never be proud, but they must never forget who they work for and the purpose that He has for them to fulfill. I can't be proud of the fact that I am a preacher because I didn't call me. I should be humbled by it. But I must never forget who I am, what I am, and what God expects of me.

The third thing is "God called *you.*" Don't attempt to be anyone else. We have great preachers and if we are not careful we will try to do it like they did it, say it like they did it, have their mannerisms, all of that. If God wanted another one of them, He would've made another one of them. *He* called *you.* So all you have to do is focus on *you* being a preacher, *you* being a child of God, *you* being what God wants you to be. Understand that God doesn't have cookie-cutter preachers. Be yourself in your development and grow to be like Jesus Christ. God called me to preach in the confines of my personality. I cannot pastor like somebody else because I am not somebody else. I cannot preach like somebody else because I am not them. God understands that I am different than everyone else. He will use me with my gifting and abilities, according to my personality.

Who has made the biggest impact on you as a preacher?

All of us are impacted by people who are very close to us. The preacher I happened to be the closest to was my father. My father never sat me down and said, "Ok, we are going to have a lesson on preaching. I am going to teach you something about preaching." That never happened. When I was a kid growing up, he may or may not have recognized that God had His hand on my life. But he would encourage me to get involved in training situations that would benefit me if I ultimately became a preacher. When I was in high school, I had no desire to type or take speech. But he would say, "Why don't you go ahead and take that class, because no matter what business you get involved with, you will be above the rest of the guys in that business if you know how to speak and type. If you can type for yourself you won't have to wait on a secretary to have time for you." That was his approach. Not surprisingly, those two skills, for example, put me way down the road in knowing how to build a sermon. It was stuff like that. It was his life, the way he lived. It was his integrity that impacted me the most.

Guy Roam was my pastor when I lived in St Louis as a teenager. Guy Roam was not the greatest preacher. But anytime anybody wants to talk about great men, his face is one of the first ones that flashes through my mind. He was always kind. He was always a Christian. He always had time for people who had nothing to offer. I will never forget the times after church as he would visit around with various people. Eventually I would get my turn to shake his hand. He was never in a hurry. He would stand there with his hands in his pockets, and talk about whatever happened to come up. He always had time. For a young man, you can't put that in words. Here is a guy that is a district superintendent. He was trying to get Gateway College off the ground. He poured his life into getting Gateway going. He would travel all over the district raising funds. That is probably one reason he wasn't a great preacher. He was so passionate about the district and about Gateway that he was traveling all over the country raising money. He didn't really have time to study. Not to mention, he had to prepare up to five sermons a week. We had church on Tuesdays, Thursdays, Saturdays, Sunday mornings and Sunday nights. That is five sermons in a week. Nobody can do that. He would preach some of the same things over and over again. Yet despite all of that, the church grew. Not because he was a great preacher but because he was a great man.

How does a preacher keep from losing sight of their calling?

The only way you can do that is to spend time with the One who called you. The apostles in Acts became distracted by church activities, and they realized they were being distracted. Once they realized what was happening, they refocused. They said, "We need to spend more time in the Word and we need to spend more time praying." That's all that matters. A preacher must do those two things. We may impress people with how much activity we do. They say, "Oh pastor you are so busy." We can really impress them with that. But you move people with prayer and with the Word. I can change people a little by creating a bunch of ministries. I have done this. I have been down that road. We are not the biggest church in the United Pentecostal Church, but I would challenge you to find a church that has more ministries, activities, and places to get involved. However, I have come to the conclusion that these things didn't really change anyone. It just made them all busy. We are already busy enough. I don't need a busy church. I need a spiritual church.

If I am going to truly change people's lives, I need to have a spiritual church. The only way to have a spiritual church is for us to pray. I have to fight for that time to pray. It doesn't come natural. You have to set aside time to pray just like you have to set aside time for anything else in ministry. The most important thing I can do is make time to pray. I have to tell folks, "Do not call me between these times. I will not answer my phone." "What are you doing, Pastor?" "I am doing the most important thing I can do: pray."

If I pray, I won't lose sight of my calling. If I don't pray, I will always lose sight of my calling.

INTERVIEW

JANET TROUT

Below are comments taken from an interview with Janet Trout, pastor of Truth and Life Center of Georgetown (Georgetown, Delaware), on the topic of the high calling of the preacher:

Do you feel there is a disconnect for some preachers today between their calling and their lifestyle?

That would have to be answered on an individual basis. You could look at a preacher who has been pastoring for thirty years; but he has a cabin on the lake, a fishing boat, and rods and reels or lots of guns to use for hunting. He's a good pastor. He's a preacher. But you could misjudge him and say there's a disconnect between his calling and his lifestyle. But that isn't always a fair assumption.

If there is disconnect—or in the case of a disconnect in today's preachers between their calling and the way they live their lives—it would be that perhaps they are misguided in the purpose of preaching.

How important is the life of the preacher in connection to their calling?

The life of the preacher and his calling are joined at the hip. They cannot be separated. If you separate the life of the preacher from his calling, one of them is going to die. This is just an observation—and I am open to a counterpoint—but I have observed over the years, preachers who seem to be so in love with their own voice, their own sound from the pulpit, their own style of preaching, and they are somewhat flattered by those who copy or mirror them. I think we might have an ego problem there.

This probably needs to be broken down and examined, especially among young preachers who are trying to find themselves and are determining the purpose of preaching, and how it is connected with their lives. Because this is a huge hazard for a preacher who loves the sound of his or her voice, and loves the adulation, and the popularity. This becomes an ego problem and it will get in the way sooner or later. A lot of times you'll see these guys or girls just blaze up to the top of the star chart, and then you'll see them like a falling star in the night just disappear; and nobody ever hears from them again.

I think the art of preaching, the practice of preaching, the purpose of preaching, the lifestyle connected to the preaching . . . these are all things that are interconnected and I don't really see how they can be disconnected.

How important is preaching today in the twenty-first century?

We need to revisit how the old-timers preached. That is, those old-timers who actually got the kind of results that we need. In other words, tell me, in the last forty sermons you've heard, how many of them have been salvation-oriented? How many of them had a high point of conviction, where the Spirit of God gripped the congregation and people literally stood up out of their seats and made their way to the altar sobbing? How many of those forty actually resulted in people going to the baptismal tank and receiving the Holy Ghost at the altar or in the baptismal tank?

I am personally calling for an old-fashioned return to an old-fashioned style that is anointed. Preachers are called to do that and must do everything necessary to make the sermon effective. They must be fasting, praying, and seeking God for the anointing. They need to select a simple topic, know when the audience gets it, and then shut it down and give an altar call.

I think it is important as long as we can retrieve the old-fashioned anointed preaching that gets the kind of results we are looking for.

What would you say to a group of next-generation preachers?

Study like it all depends on them and pray like it all depends on God. Other than that, I would tell them to be not bivocational, but probably trivocational or even more. Now this is a broad and general statement, and perhaps unfair, but many of today's preachers are so focused on their ability to walk into the pulpit, slay the congregation, and then walk out with the slaps on the back and the "That was great, brother!" compliments. As a result, that is all they can do.

I will also say, first of all, you need to go to school. You need some skills. You need accounting skills. You need some organizational management skills. You need some legal skills, to know how to stay out of trouble and how to build your ministry in a way that will never be questioned ethically or legally. You need skills that can earn a living for your family, so that you are not dependent on your preaching skills. Because many of the preachers who are out there today think they can't be effective if they are not starving their family. That is the biggest misconception I've ever seen.

In my own life, during the process of being multivocational, I have not only learned by experience; but I have been forced to go back to school to study and learn the skills to do what I am doing, and I have brought those skills to the kingdom.

So I would say to every young preacher today, you need to get your education—it needs to be broad-based and general—and learn to do kingdom work, because preaching is the easiest part of ministry. It's the easiest part to do. And if you have any public speaking skills at all, you can actually pull this thing off without anointing. If you have the ability to be a "motivational speaker," you can actually step into the pulpit of a church, sweep people off their feet, get the slaps on the back and the "That was great, brother!" compliments, and yet it was totally void of anointing.

It honestly frightens me. Because of the environment in which this new generation of preachers finds themselves, they seem to be so focused on "learning how to preach" that some of them need to be set down and told, "Listen to me Bro. I've got some things I need to tell you." And I do that by the way to my staff preachers. Preaching is the easy part.

To be an effective preacher—if preaching is your calling and you want it to be productive—you need to be trained in other skills. People who only preach live in a cocoon. They live in a shielded world. They are consumed with their own ventures. They step into pulpits and don't know how to relate to the man and wife sitting on the back pew who is on the verge of divorce. They don't know how to relate to the family who is struggling to pay their mortgage. They don't know how to relate to the teenager who is sitting in the back texting while they are preaching.

How can a preacher relate to a multigenerational congregation (young kids, young adults, middle-aged, baby boomers, and elderly)—such a broad spectrum of listeners—if they live in a cocoon and all they know to do is sign on to the computer and print off someone else's sermon and then go and spit it out like a parrot? Then they collect the tithes, gather their fishing equipment or their golf clubs and head for the lake or the golf course? Again preaching is only one aspect of ministry, and being in the pulpit is the easiest part.

How does somebody truly embrace their calling and keep from losing sight of it?

First of all, don't rent a pulpit. If you are sitting in a church, as a preacher, and that is not your church or your pulpit . . . You say, "I pay my tithes and he knows I am called to preach, so I should get a chance." I call that "renting a pulpit." And I don't think it is a very worthy goal. I do believe churches need staff ministers. We have them—four on our staff. But, I'm going to tell you, I worry sometimes about staff preachers. Where are they teaching their home Bible studies? When was the last time they brought someone to the altar and prayed them through to the Holy Ghost? It is important to get people to that altar, filled with the Holy Ghost, discipled, and then send them out as soulwinners.

To keep from losing sight of your calling, find your own pulpit. And it could be at somebody's kitchen table, teaching them a home Bible study, and leading them to the Lord.

How does one prepare for a lifetime of ministry?

Commit to walk through all open doors because one of them will lead you down the hallway you have been looking for.

What keeps a preacher from failing in ministry?

Tell the truth. Then you don't have to remember what you said. Be accountable. You have to be accountable to somebody. I am a married woman. I am seventy-five years of age. My husband is eighty years of age. And even now, when I get a call, "Come and speak. Come and preach." I always say, "Certainly, I will be happy to do that. Let me check with my husband." Even now, I am accountable to my pastor, my husband.

Ask questions and listen to your mentors. Then, have the courage to change what they point out that you may be doing incorrectly. Then monitor your results. If you are not getting results from your preaching, something may be wrong. A preacher must have results. A preacher must be productive. If there is no product, something is wrong. Either you are drowning in your own ego or you are in the wrong place, preaching to the wrong crowd. Or you have missed an open door. So what do you do to keep from failing? You have to have the courage to ask yourself the hard questions: When did I teach a Bible study last? When did I last preach someone onto their knees and into the altar? When did I last bring someone to a baptismal tank? How many people have I personally won to God in the last three months?

Finally, you have to be willing to live in a glass house. Don't be so egotistical as to believe what "I do with my private time is my business." Because, quite frankly, if you are going into the pulpit and telling other people what they should be doing with their lives, then you need to be willing to let somebody look through your window and say, "What about this?"

What are some things a preacher can begin doing today to improve their preaching?

There are two words you must remember: priorities and discipline. Anyone can set priorities, but not everyone disciplines themselves to keep their priorities. You have to set your priorities and then stay with them. Persistence breaks resistance. "Only by persistence did the snail reach Noah's ark." It wasn't his speed. It was his persistence.

Paul said, "Study to shew thyself approved unto God" (II Timothy 2:15). The flip side is also true: If you don't study you are not approved. So make up your mind what you want to be: approved or not approved. You must have good study habits. Regarding reading: Leaders are readers. I am amazed at people, including preachers who don't read. I have heard preachers say, "I don't read anything but the Bible," and their preaching reflected it. You have to know what is going on in your contemporary world.

I encourage young preachers to study the doctrine of the Trinity. If you are going to preach for or against something, you need to know what you are talking about. You don't need to read what you like to read. You should read what you don't like to read: it will stretch you.

When I started preaching, I made a vow to the Lord that I would not go to sleep at night until I had, within my limited way, mastered three chapters of the Bible. I had a few books, commentaries, and concordances, I would pour over. It took me about three and a half years. I was alright until I got to Psalm 119 and I was up until four in the morning, but I kept that vow. I fell into that kind of habit early in my walk with God.

II

SERMON PREPARATION

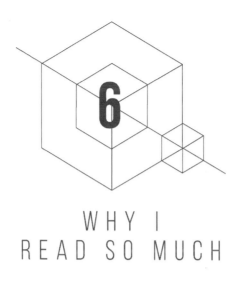

WHY I READ SO MUCH

Preachers who read widely
will most likely become better preachers.
—Cornelius Plantinga Jr.

Not all readers are leaders, but all leaders are readers.
—Harry S. Truman

The discipline of reading is crucial to the growth and development of the preacher. For some, reading is pure enjoyment. They have no trouble going from book to book, soaking in the information and gleaning the nuggets that increase their knowledge on various subjects. For me, growing up, books were pure drudgery. I would much rather play something or watch something than read something. Reading was what you did at school; and when I was home, I did not want anything to do with school.

Thankfully, I have learned the value of reading. I admit that I do enjoy it much more today than I ever have in my life. While reading is still a challenge and chore for me to do consistently, there are some things we need to do whether we like it or not.

The discipline of reading is not going to come easy to every preacher. For those who have difficulty slowing down enough to read books, stories, articles, and other beneficial materials, they need to realize it is necessary for sustained growth over a lifetime. Your motivation may not come from within. Instead, you may have to motivate yourself from without, based on your understanding that, without reading, you will struggle with depth in your preaching.

The most interesting people are oftentimes the ones with the most extensive knowledge and experience. Preaching is dependent upon both. The most interesting and effective preachers are those who are widely read, know the Scriptures well, and have firsthand experience of God's sovereign work because of what He has done in their lives through many different situations.

As a young preacher, you cannot hurry experience; but you can quickly escalate your level of knowledge through reading. Yes, true depth comes from both knowledge and experience. But those who lack experience can still be interesting and be able to share something of substance if they will take the time to develop a discipline of reading.

One word of caution: learn to read critically. In other words, don't take everything you read outside the Word of God as gospel. If possible, measure everything you read with the Bible. On the other hand, don't be afraid of being challenged in your faith. Not everything you read is going to be something you agree with. That's fine. In fact, many times you will be challenged to dig deeper and discover the why behind your faith. If you hold firm to God's Word, no idea or subject can shake you from that foundation. God's Word has been challenged for centuries upon centuries and has stood the test of time. It's not going to fall apart now because some wise guy thinks he has found a chink in God's armor.

"The grass withereth, the flower fadeth: but the word of our God shall stand forever" (Isaiah 40:8).

One of the greatest reasons preachers need to read is the fact they are pouring out what is in them on a weekly basis. Before long, if you do not put in, you will have nothing to pull out.

Of course, some preacher is going to argue that when Jesus sent the seventy out in Matthew 10, He told them not to worry about what they were going to say because the Holy Spirit would give them the words to say.

This promise was given in the context of being arrested, not preaching. Matthew 10:19 says, "But when they deliver you up (when they arrest you), take no thought how or what ye shall speak: for it shall be given you in that same hour what ye shall speak."

How often are you arrested? If at some point you are arrested, like the apostles, because of what you are preaching, then maybe you can lean on God's promise to His disciples. But until then, you better read, read, read, and then read some more. You cannot run on empty and then depend on God to come through for you. You need to give Him something to work with.

INTERVIEW

WITH

JEFF ARNOLD

Below are comments taken from an interview with Jeff Arnold, pastor of The Pentecostals of Gainesville (Gainesville, Florida), on the topic of reading and preaching:

I usually have anywhere from three to five books that I carry with me as I go throughout my day. I have a couple restaurants where I have my own booth. The waitress brings me some iced tea and lemons and I will sit there for a good hour and a half and study.

As I turn around here and look at my wall, I have wall to wall books here. I have probably read every book on my shelves.

When it comes to books, the man who impacted me was Brother Tommy Craft. One day he visited me in my motor home and noticed that I must have had fifty books on magic. When he looked at those books, he said, "What is all that stuff, Arnold?" I said, "Those are all books on magic. Yeah, I learned this from a guy in Baltimore that for two dollars I could buy twenty years of a man's life. And he looked at me and smiled and said, "That's exactly why you need to do that with reading. You can buy twenty years of a man's life."

He said, "All that stuff that you read in those books do you do it?" I said, "No, a lot of stuff I don't like, and I don't even bother with it." He said, "That's what you do when you read books (while studying for preaching/teaching, etc.); you take the good and throw away the bad."

He really helped me. So I developed an avid desire for reading quite a cross-section.

I love to read. I like A. W. Pink. I don't agree with everything, especially his thoughts on salvation, but I love his book on Genesis. I take the good and throw away the bad. There are books I like to read even though I can't preach anything out of it. I am a great fan of A. W. Tozer. Tozer was influenced by A. B. Simpson who started the Christian Alliance church and he had been miraculously healed from a breathing disease. His ministry for thirty plus years was all about healing, miracles, signs, and wonders. He was Tozer's mentor, though Tozer didn't buy into or practice those things. I also found out that Tozer came under the influence of F. F. Bosworth who was with Seymour from California. He was impacted by Bosworth's moving of faith and healing the sick, but he didn't very often practice it.

Now, I don't want anybody to get ticked off, but most preachers don't care about digging anything out; they just want a sermon. They ask me, "Hey Arnold. What are you preaching?" I tell them some things, they go preach it, and people get the Holy Ghost. I preach it and my church splits. It's like, what in the world am I doing wrong here?

I think one of the reasons I read so much is because I don't think one person knows it all. I think God gives nuggets of truth to people that are lost and are in false doctrine. But God wants those principles brought out so they put them in books and people read them.

When I start reading guys and they get off a little, I just scan it and skip over it. If you are not careful, those subtle, subliminal messages will get into the minds of millions of people, "because 'big name author' said it, God said it." You have to be discerning concerning what you read. That's what I do as I read every day. I say, "Lord, help me. If there is something here that can help me be a better Christian and give me understanding, let it quicken to me; and if not, then just let it pass."

There are some that I read that I enjoy and they challenge me. I don't preach it, but they challenge me and impact me.

What kind of books do you recommend preachers read that you don't think they read?

A. W. Pink, *Gleanings in Genesis*. Study books are crucial.

John Phillips, *Exploring Genesis* and *Exploring Psalms*. He used to be an instructor at Moody Bible School.

G. Campbell Morgan. He is one of my favorite authors, though you have to watch out for some of the things he says. *The Westminster Pulpit* is a five volume set that is really good. One book I think every preacher ought to have next to his Bible is Morgan's *The Great Physician*.

W. Phillip Keller, *Rabboni: Which Is to Say, Master*.

F. B. Meyer to me is the greatest character writer ever. There is one book he has that is worth the rest of your life: *Israel, A Prince with God*.

These guys to me were students. They weren't just trying to preach sermons, they were students. Some authors may only be about as deep as an inch of sand, but they do have some great things to say. I don't preach much of them because it is shallow, but they can give you some good insight and will help you look at things differently.

INTERVIEW

WITH

JERRY DEAN

Below are comments taken from an interview with Jerry Dean, pastor of The Pentecostals of Bossier City (Bossier City, Louisiana), on the topic of reading and preaching:

I probably read somewhere between twelve and twenty books a year. If you read only a chapter a day in a book, you can read a book every two weeks. I usually read my Bible first. I have a habit of reading a good one-year Bible program each year. Usually I will try a new translation. This year I am reading through the ESV.

We must read the Bible. Jesus said, "The words that I speak unto you they are spirit and life." I need both. Solomon said that God's Word is health to my bones. I need health.

Why do you read so much?

I read because I need knowledge. Hosea said, "My people are destroyed for lack of knowledge." It is not demons or spirits that destroy us, but a lack of knowledge. One writer said that Satan's greatest fear is our discovery of the Word of God.

I also read because I am not the best original thinker. This isn't one of my giftings; so I am constantly reading and looking for ideas. However, when reading the Bible, you shouldn't just be reading to get sermon ideas. It is our daily manna from heaven and we cannot survive without it. Read the Bible for strength, insight, and to hear the voice of God.

How do you find time to read?

I have to make time. If someone can have a set time and a special place to read, this is the best way to make reading a habit. Being a pastor makes this difficult because of so many varying interruptions.

Mark Twain said something like this, a man who doesn't read is no better off than a man who can't read.

What do you like to read?

I enjoy reading all kinds of books, but my preference is for the classics. I especially love writers like Leonard Ravenhill and E. M. Bounds. I enjoy reading Philip Yancey's books because he makes me think. I am careful not to recommend his books to anyone who is not grounded in truth.

I really enjoy reading biographies and especially biographies of our Oneness preachers. Books like *The Phenomenon of Pentecost* is an example. Last week I read the biography of Sis. Vesta Mangun's father affectionately known as Popsy Gibson. Reading these books challenges me to understand how far removed we are from sacrifice and the supernatural.

Money, Possessions, and Eternity by Randy Alcorn, and *The Wealth Conundrum* by Ralph Doudera really helped to give me a great perspective on wealth. These books are heavy in the Scripture which makes them valuable to me.

This may seem strange, but I have gleaned much from many of the small books written by Mike Murdock. I love his short chapters and appreciate his heavy use of the Bible.

I think I have all of David Bernard's books in my possession and have used them over and over to help me with my Bible Studies.

I really hate that Marvin Treece was not able to complete his commentaries before his health failed. That would have been a treasure.

The Hole in the Gospel by Richard Stearns changed the way I think toward the social gospel and prompted me to start some new programs in our church. I think it is a must read for every preacher.

I have also really enjoyed American History books. I have probably read at least ten on Lincoln.

How do you stay motivated to preach on a regular basis even when you are tired, stressed, or just plain lacking the "want to"?

Life is not about doing what you want to do, but what you ought to do. There are a lot of things we do that we don't particularly want to do. You just have to stay after it. Jesus said "If a man puts his hand to the plow and looks back, he is not fit for the kingdom." Why didn't he say "heart"? Because there are times when you put your hand to the plow because it is the thing you are supposed to do. But your heart is not there. Just keep doing it and your heart will follow your hand. You just do it because it is the thing to do.

Jesus himself, the Bible says, came apart and rested. (See Mark 6:31.) I tell preachers that if you don't come apart for a time, you are going to come apart for a long, long, time. There is nothing wrong with saying I need to back off. Taking time out to sharpen the sickle is not wasted. There are times when you need to back off and rest; regroup.

People that work a job don't feel like getting up every Monday morning. But I would hate to think we are more motivated by money than we are by a call from God. They get up and go because they have to pay bills. Every now and then you have to self-start. You don't run at the same speed all the time. Life comes in seasons. There are seasons in ministry. I am in a different season of ministry now. You have to recognize what season you are in. There are different things that happen at different seasons of life. You are not always green and have a lot of fruit. Sometimes the winter comes and you are stripped to the bare limbs. But if you hang in there and are faithful the sap will rise again and there will be some more fruit.

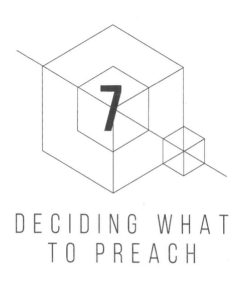

DECIDING WHAT
TO PREACH

"Preachers are physicians who, having found that the Spirit's healing arts have worked for them, are trying to take the cure to the world."[22]

One of the biggest questions young preachers have when they are asked to preach is, "What should I preach about?" Of course, the short answer is "Jesus." However, all of us from time to time struggle with settling on that one thought, idea, and Scripture we should communicate to the church. At the beginning of our ministry, we may become stressed because we haven't developed consistent preaching habits.

When I first set out evangelizing in the late nineties, I only had about five sermons. That sure made choosing what to preach a lot easier. Everything went smooth until I was preaching in Louisiana in the middle of July. After a great week-long revival, the pastor asked me to stay an extra week. That was a problem. I did not have any sermons left. It is amazing how many messages you can create when you have to. I can honestly say today that some of the best messages I ended up preaching while I evangelized came from that second week of revival when I had to work and dig out brand new messages.

When I became youth pastor, the challenge of preparing one message a week became a huge deal for me. After a couple months I had exhausted the fifteen to twenty messages I used evangelizing. Now I had to figure out how to get in a routine of preparing new sermons each and every week. It was during this time where I learned the value of planning ahead. I realized that God could speak to me a few weeks out, and I didn't need to wait until the last minute for God to let me in on what He wanted to say to the young people I was pastoring.

When I became pastor, the pressure of creating new messages each week went to a whole new level. It is one thing having to develop one, two, or even three messages a week. But having to decide what to preach each of those times is work in and of itself. Planning ahead certainly helps lighten the load. Here are a few things that are important for the preacher to consider when determining what to preach.

Sermons must be both biblical and relevant. There are three ways to make sure the sermons you preach fulfill those two requirements.[23]

The sermon must be about Jesus. On the heels of his comments about the "foolishness of preaching," Paul explained to the Corinthian church the content of that preaching:

Jews demand signs and Greeks look for wisdom, but we preach Christ crucified: *a stumbling block to Jews and foolishness to Gentiles, but to those whom God has called, both Jews and Greeks, Christ the power of God and the wisdom of God* (I Corinthians 1:22-24; emphasis mine).

Paul gave no apologies for the content of every one of his messages—Christ crucified. Jesus should be the thread woven throughout each message you preach. You may preach about David, but somehow Jesus must show up (and not in the five stones: J-E-S-U-S). God should be the hero of every Bible story we tell. We want people to have some of the characteristics of David, but we would much rather people become more like Jesus.

Preaching Jesus should be the purpose and intent of the sermon. This will come naturally from a preacher whose life is held captive by the presence of Jesus Christ. To preach Jesus is to place within the sermon the preacher's own admiration, love, and reverence for Jesus. Preaching Jesus means we will also build in Jesus' own altar appeal. People will change much more quickly when they are challenged by the commands of Jesus Christ than they will with any other kind of appeal.

The sermon must be biblical. First of all, the foundation of your preaching must never change. We have already determined that true preaching takes place only when the Bible is being communicated. You are not preaching if you are not preaching the Bible. When you are out of ideas and are desperately searching for something to preach, look in the Bible. Too often when preachers get stuck and do not know what to preach, they look on their bookshelves for inspiration.

Certainly, reading a variety of genres helps keep the preacher well-rounded. But the leadership or self-help section of your bookshelf is not the place to turn when you are dry and in need of inspiration. When you are looking for food to feed your flock, look to the milk and meat of the Word.

The sermon must be about the listeners and the present moment. The audience—their needs, questions, and struggles—must be considered when deciding on a sermon to develop. When balanced with the other two (being about Jesus and the Bible), you are better able to make a true connection to the heart of your audience.

What is happening in the community around you that may be affecting the thoughts of your congregation? What is happening in the life of the church that may be weighing on people's minds? What is the present condition, as you know it, of your church youth group? What is the present condition, as you know it, of the overall health of your church? What is presently happening in the lives of the families of your church?

It is also important to understand the life cycle and seasons of the church. There are times when victory needs to be preached. There are times when commitment needs to be stressed. There are seasons when you need to preach about healing and comfort, while there are other seasons you need to preach conviction and consecration. In every season, preaching the gospel is always appropriate.

God's timing is impeccable. It is amazing how God can take a message that becomes something spoken and delivered at just the right time. Sometimes we may not really know how to adequately diagnose our audience. This is when we learn to rely on prayer.

What am I feeling in prayer? The best preaching takes place because the preacher first felt the leading of the Spirit before he or she advised. We don't always advise listening to our feelings, but there are times when it is appropriate. When determining what to preach, ask yourself, "What am I feeling in prayer?"

As you pray throughout the week for your congregation and the families God has called you to shepherd, pay attention to how the Spirit leads you to pray for them. At times, themes will arise in your prayers over your congregation. These may be clues concerning what you should preach to them.

Meditate on Scripture while in prayer. Joining the power of prayer with the authority of the Word can produce inspiration and revelation regarding a word that needs to be communicated to the church. The psalmist prayed that God would open his eyes so that he may be able to see wonderful truths in God's law. (See Psalm 119:18.) When we pray and meditate on the Word, God will speak clearly and distinctly to those who will listen.

Listen for the Spirit to prompt you. When you sense a word from the Lord and direction from the Holy Ghost, ask yourself a couple questions: "Is this just for me?" "Is this for the congregation?" "Is this for both of us?" Write your thoughts down and wait for the Lord to give you some clear direction.

Oftentimes God will first deal with the preacher about something before the message is to be shared with the congregation. However, there are some times when God is speaking a word directly to you and solely for you. I have personally preached things that later I realized were probably just for me. This isn't necessarily wrong, but we must know what the Spirit is leading us to say. Maybe that message was supposed to be for both, but it needed more time to take root in you as the preacher before you delivered it.

Some of the greatest preaching thoughts will come to you during your personal devotion time and reading of the Word. I have note pages filled with random thoughts that come to me when I am reading daily through the Word of God. Great thoughts do not come every day, but when they do come it is so refreshing.

Listen for the Spirit to talk to you while you are reading God's Word. If you are not on a daily reading plan or if you have not yet developed a habit of reading God's Word on a daily basis, you are neglecting the power God has made available to you. In addition, you are short-changing congregants who are depending upon you to stay in tune with what God is saying to His church through His Word.

Planning Ahead. As a pastor, learning to plan ahead will be one of the greatest gifts you can give yourself. Some preachers have struggled with the idea of God being able to anoint anything that isn't done at the last minute. "I can't plan what I am going to preach next month because God may change His mind." I believe we can pray and seek God about what He will have us preach next month because He is already there. He knows who will be in the service. He knows what needs will be present. And He knows how to anoint you in your study in March for a message in May.

You can develop sermons from a variety of different planning methods:

A study on a book of the Bible—many pastors and congregations have found preaching through a whole book of the Bible to be very fulfilling. Being able to see the whole book in context is sometimes more enlightening to a preacher and the congregation than preaching randomly from one or two verses of a chapter.

While pastoring, I preached through the book of Acts—a series I entitled: *Our Apostolic Heritage.* In fact, if you have never tried it, you may be surprised at how exciting this can be. When you and your congregation go through a book of the Bible together, the purpose of the author comes alive. Oftentimes, congregants will find themselves learning much more during one of these studies than they do in six months' worth of topical sermons.

A topical sermon series—developing a series is a great way to take time building on a topic that is too big to cover in one service. Many preachers and pastors will take the beginning of the year to deliver a series that sets the tone for the vision of the church for that year. Other important biblical themes can be given the proper coverage when a preacher takes a few weeks to preach it.

I also enjoyed preaching sermon series when I pastored. One year, I preached through the month of January on our year's theme: *Following the Fire.* The series followed the children of Israel and their wilderness wanderings outlined in the book of Exodus. Here were my four sermon titles: 1. Life in a Tent, 2. Willing to Follow, 3. Ready to Follow, 4. No More Wandering. I set a tent up on the platform and the series really helped the church come together with purpose for the new year.

Current Events—though it is not recommended to constantly preach from the newspaper, it is beneficial for the church when the pastor expresses a biblical response to current events from time to time. Current event sermons can be great opportunities to show your people the relevance of Scripture in today's world.

When the market crashes, when war is declared, when Hollywood produces something controversial (well, that happens just about every day), or when a tragedy hits close to home, your congregation wants to know what the Bible has to say about these things. As preachers, we may not personally have answers for everything, but the Bible will have something to say.

The Calendar—Easter, Mother's Day, Father's Day, and other special days are important in the life of the church. What are the special days in the life of your own church? The pastor will find many of these special days lend themselves to fairly obvious sermon topics and ideas.

In fact, many of these days are actually times when once-a-year churchgoers decide to join us for service. These are great opportunities to influence them and encourage them to consider making Jesus a part of their lives. Yes, it is difficult sometimes when the "holiday spirit" settles on your congregation, and it feels like no one is really all that engaged in what is going on. Still, we can't let that bother us. It does not remove our responsibility and the mandate we have to preach the truth of God's Word.

Sermon Seed File—if you do not have a file (digital or physical) where you store random thoughts, ideas, and illustrations, start one today. Many who have preached for years have some sort of system they have developed to collect thoughts for future sermon material. If not, you are missing out on a great resource for those moments when you are searching for something to preach.

Many times I have pulled out my files of random thoughts I had written down while I read Scripture or sat in a service listening to someone preach. It was refreshing to read these ideas as they helped jumpstart my mind and give me some direction as I began preparing something to preach.

INTERVIEW

STAN GLEASON

Below are comments taken from an interview with Stan Gleason, assistant general superintendent of the United Pentecostal Church, and pastor of The Life Church (Kansas City, Missouri) on the subject of deciding what to preach:

How do you know what to preach?

I don't know that there is really one surefire way to determine this. Hindsight is always 20/20. Number one, you can't judge whether you were in the will of God or whether you made the right decision on what to preach based on how you felt while you were preaching, how you felt when you were done with the message, or even on the visible feel-good results of your message. You never know.

Someone recently commented to me on a message I had preached ten years ago. They said, "You have no idea how that really helped me." Now, I distinctly remember where I was and what I was thinking when I preached that message years ago. I thought, "I didn't help anybody with that." We say "we are just the mailman," and so we are. We just deliver what God gives us.

I have had the Lord speak to me in prayer—though it doesn't happen every week—about a specific word to share with the church. Oftentimes, thoughts and messages surface while seeking the Lord in prayer and studying of the Scriptures. If you don't study, pray, and read, you will have a harder time.

There is a message I preached several years ago for the first time that I have now preached all over. When I prepared that message, I knew I had heard from God. But when I was going over it right before the service I began to have my doubts. However, it was the only message I had. I had no other choice but to go with it. But now, when I think about the impact of that message and how I felt about my choice beforehand, I would've never connected those dots. But while I was preaching I knew I had heard from God.

Is there that one right message that must be preached on any given Sunday?

The answer to that is "yes" and "no." There are occasions where there has to be a word from God. The church is at a crossroads. We have had some of those landmark messages. There was a preacher who recently preached for me and he told our church this: "I went to the General Conference in Toronto in 2003. I was distraught, hurt, and frustrated. But your pastor preached at the General Conference: 'You Can Trust the Body.' It was like a balm washed over my soul. It sent a wave of peace across this movement."

As a general rule, I don't think there is only one message for one specific moment for one specific time. I don't really know that it is so important what you preach as long as you are flowing with the Spirit and working with the anointing. You can preach on "money" and people get healed. You can preach on "faith" and people give money. It is biblical and anointed and God can meet any need out there through the power of the Word of God. What God ends up doing in the lives of people during that service and at the end of your preaching doesn't even necessarily have to do with what you preach about.

A pastor once told me about a situation in which his wife was deathly sick but kept saying, "Oh if I can just get to church and hear the Word of God." They literally carried her to church and laid her on the front pew. The preacher in the pulpit didn't even preach on healing. But by the time he was finished preaching, that pastor's wife was up on her feet worshiping the Lord. It's because of the nature of God's Word. It is a book of revelation.

I have learned that the important thing is to put your best effort forth and flow in the anointing. God will take care of it all.

What are some things preachers can begin doing today to improve their preaching?

Read as many non-fiction books as you can get your hands on. Read. Read. Read. Read a wide variety of subjects. I recommend the *Smithsonian* magazine. I used to receive this and when I would receive these, every month the magazines would be full of subjects I had never heard of and didn't even care about. I would read it anyway. And now I've been educated a little bit on a wide variety of subjects and have discovered that things I knew nothing about or had never even heard of were extremely interesting. These subjects would open up a whole new world for me. The reason for reading a variety of subjects is: I cannot preach what I don't know. He can best use me according to how big a pool of information or knowledge I have to work from. So read all the time on as many subjects as you can get your hands on. Read for sermon preparation and read to keep yourself from looking dumb to people in the world. When they bring up a subject and you know something about it that will dispel what the world is trying to make them think about preachers. "This preacher is knowledgeable. He knows more than just John 3:16. He knows something about what I know about." Then you have credibility.

The second thing is to spend time with preachers that challenge you and inspire you to be a better person. Don't waste time with preachers that are negative and complaining. It doesn't take any intelligence to find something wrong with what's going on. There's always something wrong going on. Don't spend time with them because they will drag you down to their level of thinking. Always spend time with people who challenge you and who inspire you. You don't have to say anything. You may be intimidated by being around them. But just stand there and listen. Listen to what they say and talk about. Preachers are going to talk about golf and hunting and various things. But after a while they are going to say some things that will turn a light on in your head. Be around those people. Go find somebody who has a relationship with God and just stand there and soak it up.

Third, spend time with God and in the Bible. I am not talking about praying for a sermon. All of us pray for a sermon. That's not praying. That's looking for a sermon. Real praying is: "God change me. God fix me. God, work on me. God, help me to be like You." When you are reading your Bible, not looking for something to preach to somebody else, but so that it will have an impact on your life, that changes you. That is going to affect everything else you do.

RESEARCHING
THE SERMON

A man from Ethiopia—in fact, an important government figure under Candace, Queen of Ethiopia—was returning from a trip. He had acquired a scroll with the prophecy of Isaiah written on its parchment. As he was riding in the royal chariot, he became engulfed in the words of the ancient seer. "Who hath believed our report, and to whom is the arm of the LORD revealed . . . But he was wounded for our transgressions, he was bruised for our iniquities, the chastisement of our peace was upon him and by his stripes we are healed." (See Isaiah 53.)

He was mesmerized by Isaiah's depiction of this suffering servant who, innocent in his own right, found himself beaten and bruised for others who had done wrong. He wondered at this man. He questioned and hungered to know what all this meant. Something within him longed for answers. We don't know how, but his internal cry for understanding reached God's throne. For at the very same moment, Philip the Evangelist was wrapping up his Samaritan crusade and baptizing his last convert in Samaria.

The Lord spoke to Philip to head south. As he walked, he noticed a chariot approaching from the east. Compelled by the Spirit to draw near to the chariot, Philip began jogging until he was running alongside the royal carriage. Noticing the man in the chariot reading from a scroll, Philip asked, "Do you understand what you are reading?"

The Ethiopian, somewhat caught off guard as he was pulled out of deep concentration, looked down at Philip and just shook his head. "Actually, no. I am not sure what this prophet is talking about." The eunuch called for the chariot to stop and invited Philip to come up and sit with him. For the next several moments, Philip began to preach to the eunuch about Jesus.

What were only words to the eunuch, were personal and had been experienced by Philip. If Philip had not spent time with Jesus, learning from the Messiah Himself, Philip would have had nothing more to add to Isaiah's writings than what the eunuch could read for himself. Philip's knowledge and understanding brought a depth to Isaiah's writings and led to spiritual revelation in the Ethiopian's heart.

Your audience should be able to trust that you know more concerning what you are talking about than they do. Yes, you may have elder saints in your church who have lived for God for seventy years, have read the Bible through a thousand times, and have taught the adult Sunday school class for the past fifty years. You may not know more than they do. But even they deserve to hear from a preacher who has done his or her best to study, research, and prepare as much as they can. If the preacher has not done the necessary study and research, they have nothing more to add than what the audience could glean for themselves by simply reading the text they heard read before them.

God's Word is a treasure that is never exhausted. The more you study, read, and research, the more you find that you never knew. And preaching from a heart and message that are well-prepared will also lead to spiritual revelation in the lives of those who hear you.

I was privileged to be a part of a ministerial alliance in a small town where I pastored. Though the town had a larger ministerial alliance that included pastors from every Christian persuasion, I was informed of another group that met weekly in addition to the larger alliance. This was a small group of local pastors who led Spirit-filled churches.

They told me about a monthly community service they had been doing for some time. Every few months, their churches would get together at a host church, and one of the pastors would preach. I was intrigued and wanted to be a part. I was honored when they asked me to preach at the first community service I would attend. I sought the Lord and wanted to deliver a message that would encourage each congregation but would also be respectful to all the pastors in attendance since our church did have a few distinct beliefs that set us apart from them. They knew this and still trusted me. That was humbling.

I chose to take my text from the Book of Exodus and talked about the wilderness wanderings of the Israelites and their encounter with the rock that gushed forth with water. I preached about the Rock. I preached about Moses speaking to the rock and water coming forth. I talked about Moses striking the rock and water coming forth. Then I took them to the New Testament and showed them that Jesus was that Rock. (See I Corinthians 10:4).

After the service, a man from one of the other churches approached me and thanked me for the message. He said, "We have been studying that very passage in the Old Testament, but had been unable to fully understand the meaning. Your message brought clarity, understanding, and revelation."

I wouldn't say that my research for that sermon was any more involved than other sermons I had preached. But growing up in a church that taught me who Jesus was—the God of the Old Testament manifest in flesh—I was able to give some insights that others there had never considered.

You can preach from an English Bible because you know what most English words mean. But knowing background, setting, authorial intent, and the connection between Old and

New Testaments, among other things, brings a whole new level of depth to a message. Even though you may never use all you find in your study and research, just having that information and understanding in your mind and spirit, will add so much to your presentation and delivery.

The audience you are preaching to is intelligent. They can tell whether you know what you are talking about or not. Build depth of knowledge and understanding whether you think you will need it or not. It shows diligence and respect—respect for your calling, your audience, and your Boss.

As a young preacher, one of the worst things you can do is underprepare. Don't just spend time preparing notes; spend time preparing your heart and mind. Immerse yourself in the text. Find out all the information you can about the text, the author, the book containing the text, the background, the setting, and the reason the author wrote those words. As you can see, this takes time. If you have adequate warning—which most of the time you will—start early and make time for the necessary preparation.

INTERVIEW

WITH

CHESTER MITCHELL

Below are comments taken from an interview with Chester Mitchell, pastor of Capital Community Church (Ashburn, Virginia), on the topic of researching the sermon:

How much time should be spent developing and researching a sermon?

I don't think there is a set amount of time. I think it depends on you. Some preachers are really strong Bible teachers. For instance, I did a series of messages covering the core doctrines of repentance, baptism, the daily struggles we face, and the empowering of the Holy Spirit. I preached out of Romans 5-8. That was a solid theological series of messages. They took me a lot longer in preparation than normal.

Messages where I cast vision, for instance, they are not as deep theologically. They may take a little less time in terms of study but they may take more emotional time figuring out how I am going to cast the vision. It depends on what you are doing. I think you just have to be prepared to put in whatever work you need to in order to be ready.

When do you know you are finished and ready to compose? How do you weed through everything and know what to use?

You must determine on the front end of your preparation, by asking yourself, "What is it you want to say?" Put that in no more than two or three sentences. Then ask, "What do you want them to do?" Those two questions are imperative. I think because we are a movement of preachers, we put too much out there in most sermons. My opinion is: "less is best." When I look out across the church I pastor, I see increasingly that I am reaching people that have very little Judeo-Christian knowledge. If I put a whole lot out there, it may sound great and it might be entertaining, but it is not practical.

I see preaching as a long term thing. I am trying to get people to Heaven and I realize that it is not going to happen this coming Sunday. So I don't have to put it all out there. I would probably be better off by saying, "OK, I want them to know these two or three things, and I want them to do these two or three things."

I think moving into the twenty-first century, our preaching needs to be much more focused. A lot of our preaching is all over the place. I think that one of the best things a preacher can do is write a paragraph encapsulating his sermon's focus—"this is what I want to talk about"—and then stick to it.

What does your weekly preparation look like?

What I try to do is come up with a theme. I do my best preaching in series. There are very few Sundays whose messages stand alone. Mother's Day, graduation Sunday, and others . . . but even those Sundays may be a part of a series. All of this is decided at least two or three months ahead. For each message of the series, I ask the question, "What is the big thing I want to get across in that message?" The week before, I will lay the format of the message out in my mind. I am an outline preacher. Every Sunday the congregation gets an outline of my message.

Monday: I write out some thoughts.

Tuesday: I come back and refine them.

Wednesday: I pretty much have my outline down on paper and hand it off to my secretary to get it formatted.

Thursday: I look it over one last time and decide, "This is what I want." By the afternoon I am done with it.

Friday: I don't think about it at all.

Saturday: I go through it one more time and add any additional thoughts I may have.

Murrell Ewing once said, "I don't go looking for sermons. They find me." I have noticed that whatever I am supposed to be preaching about, it finds me. In my prayer time, in my devotional and Bible reading time, when I am reading a book, when I am listening to another preacher, it finds me when I am spending leisure time. It finds me all over.

I live with the idea that I am a communicator of God's truth, and I am looking for those truths to find me every which way.

INTERVIEW

WITH

STAN GLEASON

Below are comments taken from an interview with Stan Gleason, pastor of The Life Church of Kansas City (Kansas City, Missouri), on the topic of researching the sermon:

Once I have settled on a thought or direction, I sit down at my computer and just start writing. I can't do that for hours on end. I know how my brain and spirit works. I get saturated and cannot stay there. This is why I try to start early. If I am going to speak on Sunday, I start working Monday. I have to sit down and start writing. I do better once I see it on the screen. I never worry about having enough material. I always have to shrink things down. I script all my messages. I always start out with the manuscript, but many times will get away from it when I preach.

My pastors Robert Sabin and S. G. Norris were so in touch with what was going on in the world, and to me, that is a big deal. People come to church to hear what you have to say about what is going on. And if you don't say it, you are missing an opportunity. The people will go somewhere to hear what someone has to say about what is happening in the world. If the elephant is in the room, we better talk about it. If a major event happens in the world that shakes society and you don't even address it on Sunday, that is foolish on your part.

How much time should be spent developing and researching a sermon?

The less experienced the speaker, the more preparation time is needed. My opinion is, no less than twenty hours for a forty minute message. The people deserve that. When you

111

multiply the man hours sitting in your audience (their time), they deserve better than just a few scraps of paper and a cheeseburger Happy Meal. They deserve better than that and so does God. I have been preaching thirty-five years, and I still spend twenty hours on some things.

Preaching has not come easy for me. I have had to dig and claw and scratch for everything I've ever gotten. I remember those early days of evangelizing. Pastors would want me to go play with them, run around to all the hospitals, or go eat at Grandma Moses' lunch table. I would tell them, "I love you, but if you want to have revival, I need to spend some time so I can get a message." I would struggle, and I would spend a minimum of twenty hours on sermon prep. But now that I am older, I would say my average prep time is about half that.

There have only been a handful of times that I have ended up preaching something different from what I went to the pulpit with. In thirty-five years that has happened no more than a half dozen times. Some would say, "Well, you don't follow the Lord." Why can't God talk to me a few days before? Why does it have to be right before the sermon? What that tells me is that I didn't hear God in the first place. It is not God's problem, it is my problem.

What does your weekly preparation look like?

I start on Monday with writing down thoughts. But I don't start word processing it until later in the week like Thursday. I try to catch it when the inspiration comes.

How do you know when you are finished preparing?

If I don't know when I am finished, that is what you call a series. Seriously though, there are some times I don't know until I am preaching the message. I have decided while preaching that I am not going to get done, and I need to make this a series.

How do you stay motivated to preach on a regular basis even when you are tired, stressed, or just plain lacking the "want to"?

This is rooted in personal consecration—staying connected with God. Some young preachers ask me, "How long do you study? When do you study? How much do you study?" What I tell them is, "24/7. If I am awake, I am studying. I never cease to study." I may not have a Bible in my hand, but I am quoting to myself memorized Scriptures. I have it in my mind and in my heart.

In Matthew 13, the Bible talks about the "good seed." For years we have taught that the seed is the Word. I have no problem with that. It is a true application. However, if you read the parable in Matthew 13, Jesus said, "The good seed are the children of the Kingdom" (Matthew 13:38). We are the seed. The preacher is the message. We talk about, "Let's get a message." No, be a message. Preaching is not what I do; it is what I am. I don't wait until Friday or Saturday and say, "I got to preach Sunday morning so I need to get something together. I need to get a message or a sermon." No, every day I am walking in it; I'm living in it.

Second, you stay motivated by having passion. You must continually fuel your passion for the kingdom of God, for the people of God, and for the cause of God. If you would boil them all down to their truest essence, your most sought after preachers are those who are known for their passion. Passion is what separates. That is the point of demarcation. Effective preaching is predicated upon the conviction of the speaker. The one that is affective is the one that truly, one hundred percent believes what they are saying. Too many say things they really don't believe themselves.

Third, is the power of the place of calling. When you are in your calling (as a pastor, evangelist, missionary, etc.), I believe there is an attending anointing and accompaniment

113

of the Spirit. There is something about being in a particular place if it is God who has placed you there. I've never seen a Sunday when I didn't want to preach. I have never thought that way. I've never struggled with, "Boy, I just don't feel like preaching today." I may not physically be feeling well, but I have never said, "I don't want to preach." The only way I think you get to that point is when you have not been praying and spiritually posturing yourself to be connected to God.

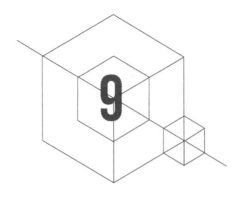

THE IMPORTANCE OF UNDERSTANDING THE PASSAGE'S IDEA

Who hasn't done something like this before?

You are looking for a word from God for a particular situation and have come to the place of desperation. You pick up your Bible, close your eyes, flip open the Book, and let your finger fall randomly onto a verse. You open your eyes to read what the Lord would say to you in your present situation. And you know, sometimes it works, sometimes it doesn't. That being said, asking God for direction from His Word is necessary; doing it blindly and randomly is not the way to go about it. You may just end up reading into a verse something it wasn't meant to communicate.

Unfortunately, when it comes to choosing texts, preachers do this all the time. They may not randomly select verses with their eyes closed, but they will often choose a text and preach a sermon explaining the text incorrectly. We understand that verse distinctions were created by translators to better organize the material, which in turn helps us, as readers, understand the text. However, in order to fully comprehend the text, we must look before and after the verse or verses we have chosen.

As someone once said, when you see the word "Therefore," you need to look at the verses preceding to understand why it is "there for." This is a catchy way of highlighting the importance of context. The preacher must look at context before verse analysis can be done properly.

Andrew Matthew, in his lecture "An Overview of Contextual Analysis" suggests we look at four different areas of context when analyzing the meaning of Biblical texts.[24]

When beginning to look at context, we must first start with the immediate context. After choosing a text, first look at the verse itself: words, names, places, etc. The preacher must not simply assume a certain word found in the verse means the same thing in the twenty-first century as it did in the first century. Find out the origin of that word, if possible. What do other translations say? Do they use the same word or another word that helps reveal what is really meant?

First Peter 3:16 says, "Having a good conscience; that, whereas they speak evil of you, as of evildoers, they may be ashamed that falsely accuse your good *conversation* in Christ."

If I am not familiar with the biblical meaning of "conversation," I will not fully understand Peter's intent in this verse. In fact, if I develop a message using this verse and have not done the proper research, I may tell my audience to not say anything that would cause others to determine you are not a true disciple of Christ. Yes, there are other verses that would probably back up that statement—it is truth and an important admonition—but this is not what Peter is saying.

A true word study will reveal even more about the origin of this word, but here, a simple glance at another translation will reveal quite a bit: "Keeping a clear conscience, so that those who speak maliciously against your good *behavior* in Christ may be ashamed of their slander" (I Peter 3:16, NIV).

"Different cultures use words in different ways and add a further challenge to the understanding when those words are translated into another language. We must recognize as well that the Bible, being written over a span of 3,500 years, has had some words change in meaning. With the original words having been translated into another language so more people could read, the Bible now presents the challenge to have all the words being translated with the same fullness of meaning from one language to another. A full understanding of the words of a text can be attained by researching the key words of any passage in theological dictionaries such as Kittle's *Theological Dictionary of the New Testament* or Colin Brown's *New International Dictionary of New Testament Theology*."[25]

After poring over the verse or verses of your text, see whether these verses are part of a larger thought from a *broader passage* or group of verses. By using the verses you have chosen, are you missing the big picture? Have you pulled three verses out of the author's stream of thought that actually covered twelve verses? Here is where you read verses before and after in order to determine the main idea.

There is no standard number of verses you will have to read before or after to determine the bigger picture. It will be different every time. Look for words that are repeated over the course of a passage to help determine the theme the author is communicating. When you understand the theme of the broader passage, it will hopefully shed light on the immediate context of the text you have chosen.

Next you will want to look at the *context of the entire book*. Using the above passage as an example, if your text comes from I Peter 3:16, you will want to do a study of the purpose and themes of the entire book of I Peter. Again, you may have a lot of information gathered from study that will never be used in your sermon, but knowing this helps build depth and lends greater credibility to the interpretation you choose to draw from the text.

Finally, the preacher needs to consider how the text fits in the *context of the entire Bible*. Does it fit into or shed light upon the overall theme of redemption and salvation, the ultimate message the Scriptures share? Beyond that, look at how or whether this theme was addressed in other books by the same author. It will also be helpful to look at how other authors present similar themes in their books. Additionally, take time to find any parallel passages from the Old Testament.

Understanding context is crucial not only for understanding the correct meaning of the text, but also for identifying the main idea of the text. Only by determining the main idea of the text (the passage idea) can we then adequately determine the main idea of our sermon (the sermon idea). If you choose to preach an expository sermon, the main idea of the passage actually becomes the main idea of your sermon.

Finding the Main Idea of the Passage

"When you look at the biblical text you can look at many things and highlight them, but there is one main idea the author wants to get across. It is essential that you get the main idea before you look at all the peripheral stuff." This is "the thesis, the overriding thought, the assertion, the summary sentence, the propositional statement, etc. Haddon Robinson calls it the Big Idea. It is the main idea the author wants to communicate."[26]

Why is it important to find the main idea of the passage? First of all, whether you are preaching an expository sermon or a topical sermon, finding the main idea is crucial. This must be the first part of your preparation process. Having a main idea is foundational for good communication to transpire. When you sit down to talk with someone, most of the time you have a purpose or idea you are trying to get across. Whether you relate a story, express emotion, talk slowly or softly, your purpose is to communicate a specific thought.

"Having a main idea is essential for understanding to take place. If you want to know whether a person understood a book they read, ask them this question, "What was the book about?" If they understood it, they can state it in a succinct sentence or series of sentences. If they can only recall a bunch of facts, figures, or images, then they have not grasped the main idea."[27]

This is clearly seen in messages where preachers have not determined their sermon idea. (See chapter 10.) They take their audiences on one short walk after another until the congregation is confused and lost, without a clear picture of what the preacher is trying to say. As humans, we want an anchoring thought or idea to hold on to as the preacher is preaching. Nothing is more unsettling than a sermon without a clear focus.

> Our minds crave unity. No one thrives in chaos. That is why we have governments and laws. It is an attempt to provide unity. That is what science is constantly doing. The astronomer looks at the mass of stars and heavenly bodies in the sky and begins organizing them into constellations and galaxies.
>
> It is no different in human communication. We seek unity. We feel a dissonance or uneasiness when a person rambles. We expect that of a person who has lost their mental abilities or hasn't gotten enough sleep. But that is the way some congregations feel as they listen to the man in the pulpit. He is rambling. The preacher thinks the audience is hanging on their every word, when in reality they are trying to make sense of all the ideas and words the preacher has thrown out.[28]

Not only do we want unity in communication, we also seek to find order. We look for a logical flow in thoughts that are being spoken. We may grasp an idea; but if we don't see how it fits in the whole, we become confused and lose interest. Understanding the whole will also allow us to remember the message much longer. I have heard interesting speeches chock full of quotes and stories that were memorable in and of themselves. But not seeing how they all fit together caused me to lose something, not to mention, the speech lost something too—its intended effect on the listeners.

How am I supposed to follow someone who is lost? Oh, they may know a few of the street names and even have a destination address; but if they do not know in what order to make each turn, they will never get to the address. This only means I don't end up where they want me to end up either. Sadly, even if the preacher ends up at the address, he or she lost so many other cars behind them on the way, the fact the preacher made it doesn't even matter.

This leads to the final point: the main idea is important because it lets the preacher know he has gotten where he wanted to go. "My preacher used to say that if you aim at nothing you will always hit it. When we communicate, I hope your target isn't 'nothing.' There is a word for communication that doesn't have a target—babble or chatter. Most of us don't enjoy babbling. When someone babbles, I will respond by saying, 'What did you say?' What I am asking them in technical terms is, 'What is your point, your main idea?'"[29]

So for preaching to be effective, the preacher must have an aim or objective in mind. What is your goal? Whatever that goal may be will determine how you choose to reach it. That objective will lead you to develop a path of ideas, thoughts, main points, illustrations, and Scripture passages linked together to get you to that end goal. If you do not have an aim or objective, you will never know if you reached it. The main idea brings focus and direction.

The biblical writers had a main idea that they wanted to communicate. It is your responsibility as the expositor to discover that main idea. You are not ready to prepare a sermon until you have discovered the main idea.

Ideas

This may sound like a simple question, but, what is an idea? Merriam-Webster can help us in a technical sense: an idea is "a thought, plan, or suggestion about what to do." To take it even further, an idea is a complete thought. Spann suggests there are two components that comprise an idea. Every idea has a subject and a complement.

If you were to ask another preacher, "What are you going to preach about on Sunday?" their response may be, "I am going to preach about faith." Of course, you respond with a Holy Ghost shrug of your shoulders, a little kick in your leg, a short "shhhew" and say, "that's good!" Then after that encouraging response to your friend, you look a little puzzled. Faith is the subject. But that is an awfully big subject. You calmly reply, "Someone could preach for weeks on end about faith and never exhaust the topic. You only have thirty minutes to preach. What are you going to say about faith?"

Faith is not a complete idea. The subject is not complete by itself. There is something else the subject needs—a complement. Instead, how about one of these:

1. Faith is necessary for salvation.
2. Without faith it is impossible to please God.
3. Faith without works is dead.

Now you have focus and can better prepare a message because you have an idea you are trying to get across.

Here are some practical steps Kent Spann suggests to take in finding the main idea of a biblical passage:[30]

Let's start with a biblical text. As an example, let's say you were reading through the book of Romans and arrived at chapter 12. As you read the first few verses, you were struck by Paul's writing, felt a witness in your spirit, and you were drawn back to the first two verses.

"I beseech you therefore, brethren, by the mercies of God, that ye present your bodies a living sacrifice, holy, acceptable unto God, which is your reasonable service. And be not conformed to this world: but be ye transformed by the renewing of your mind, that ye may prove what is that good, and acceptable, and perfect, will of God" (Romans 12:1-2).

First of all, *determine from a general reading of the text what the author is talking about.* What is the subject the author is addressing? Here you may notice we have a "therefore." This should immediately trigger a need to go back a few verses (in this instance, the previous chapter) and determine what is being talked about.

You will observe chapter 11 is discussing the remnant of Israel and how the rebellion of Israel led to the engrafting of the Gentiles into God's plan to redeem mankind. In addition, we see a theme that pops up in the last few verses that is also seen in the first two verses of chapter 12.

"As concerning the gospel, they are enemies for your sakes: but as touching the election, they are beloved for the fathers' sakes. For the gifts and calling of God are without repentance. For as ye in times past have not believed God, yet have now obtained *mercy* through their unbelief: Even so have these also now not believed, that through your *mercy* they also may obtain *mercy*. For God hath concluded them all in unbelief, that he might have *mercy* upon all" (Romans 11:28-32).

"I beseech you therefore, brethren, by the *mercies* of God, that ye . . ." (Romans 12:1, emphasis mine).

Though there may be several "general subjects" to choose, the theme of mercy stands out to me. Let's say the broad subject being talked about in this passage is "the mercy of God."

Secondly, *determine the question asked about the broad subject.*

Looking at Romans 12:1-2 and taking into account the "therefore" and the previous verses, it appears that the question being asked is, "How should we respond to God's mercy?"

Next, *convert the question into a phrase.*
"We should respond to God's mercy by . . ."

Next, *answer the question raised by the text.*

". . . by presenting our bodies to God as a living sacrifice, refusing to be conformed to this world, and allowing God to transform our thoughts and actions."

Finally, *make the question and its answer into a statement.*

We should respond to God's mercy by presenting our bodies to God as a living sacrifice, refusing to be conformed to this world, and allowing God to transform our thoughts and actions.

This seems to encapsulate Paul's thoughts and purpose for the first few verses of Romans 12. Understanding this idea, the preacher can better develop a message from the text. Though he may choose a topical message, such as preaching about "Being a Living Sacrifice," this understanding of what motivates this desire will bring greater depth and understanding to his message. He may not even mention the verses in chapter 11 and may say very little about refusing to be conformed or being transformed by the renewing of our mind. That is fine because his focus is much more narrow and centered on the topic at hand.

However, if he were going to preach an expository sermon, in order to be true to the text, he would want to include a lot of the information gathered during his search for the passage main idea. It would be important for him to include some of the verses from chapter 11 that led him to recognize the theme of mercy. A good sermon title for this expository sermon may be: "Motivated by Mercy."

Who has made the biggest impact on you as a preacher?

During my early, formative years in ministry, just coming out of Bible School, Jerry Jones was the general youth president. He is still one of the guys that every time I hear him, I go, "Wow!" I told him one time, "When you preach I run this gamut of emotions. In one breath I get inspired and say 'I want to learn to preach.' But then the next minute I shake my head and think 'I'm never gonna be able to preach.'" He has made a big impact on me both because of his skills in the pulpit and the timing in my life. I've told the same thing to Mike Williams. He challenges me with the use of words. I watch a guy who is such a wordsmith, such a poet. He made me want to expand my vocabulary and do better.

Although he was a great preacher, someone who really impacted me beyond the pulpit was James Kilgore. He touched my life, though he didn't know it. In a very broken moment, when I was very young, he sat beside me on a couch and cried till he had wet spots from tears dripping off his cheeks onto both of his pant legs. He didn't even know me. He had never seen me before that day. But I was just a broken young man and he was broken with me. Now in that moment, I was too consumed with my own issues and problems to really grasp the magnitude of that, but later I thought, "Yeah, there's a reason a thousand people called him pastor." The compassion he showed me really moved me. It was less about "pulpiteering." But the character of ministry in that man has affected me for life.

THE IMPORTANCE OF
DEVELOPING
THE SERMON IDEA

One of the most oft quoted pieces of advice on preaching bears repeating: "If you cannot summarize your sermon in one concise sentence, then you are not ready to preach it."

It is difficult to construct a sermon around more than one main idea. Without a clear sermon idea, the message itself will probably go a handful of different directions and leave the audience without a clear understanding of what the preacher was trying to say.

Our goal in preaching is not to just articulate information and facts. We want to see lives changed. A good sermon idea will enable the hearers to take the sermon with them and apply it. I would venture to say that a well-developed sermon idea will be your best friend in the pulpit.

Once you have studied your text and the context of the passage in which it is found, your next step is to develop the sermon idea. Again, this sermon idea is what you are saying as a preacher. What is the one thing you want your audience to take away from this message? What idea are you trying to drive home? The sermon idea gives the preacher focus in helping him hone the parts of the message into one complete thought, illustrated by a couple different points.

It should be noted that this process can take a little time. It will not always come easy. If it did, preachers would take the time to create this for every sermon. But the fact it takes time and work seems to push preachers away from this important practice. One of the reasons it takes time is because it should be a carefully worded statement.

"The preacher who wants to be an effective communicator must become a wordsmith."[31] Merriam-Webster says a word-smith is "a person who works with words." He is an expert with words. A carpenter will work will all kinds of tools: hammers, saws, tape measures, and levels. But a preacher works with words. Words are his tools.

It matters how you say something. This is why thoughts and ideas must not simply be thrown out without regard for how they are verbally constructed. How many good thoughts or ideas do we waste or decrease their impact because we haphazardly toss them out without regard to verbal presentation?

The preacher must work with words until he is able to craft a statement that accurately and powerfully sums up the idea of the sermon as a whole. This requires sweat and hard work. There will be times the sermon idea jumps out at you like a cricket from a book, while at other times you feel like you are searching for water in a desert.

The sermon idea should be constructed with the audience in mind. Also, like the passage idea, it should have a subject and a complement. (See chapter 9.) And though some may disagree, I believe the sermon idea should be written in a complete sentence. Phrases are not always complete ideas. Do not confuse this with your sermon title. Perhaps the title will reflect or mimic your sermon idea, but the title is something completely different.

The sermon title is a short phrase—or at times only a few words—that serves as a label for the sermon. It gives the audience a handle to hold onto while riding in the vehicle of the sermon. Often, they will work hand in hand, but they each serve a different purpose.

Dr. Kent Spann gives a few suggestions that will help your audience grasp the sermon idea:[32]

1. State the sermon idea in the most memorable sentence possible.

Be creative. Don't be wordy. Be concise.

2. State it for the ear, since preaching is oral and not written communication.

If you were writing a book or an article, you would probably construct your thought a little differently. However, you are trying to communicate to people who are listening to your voice. This is why alliteration and the use of simple, straightforward language is important.

3. State the sermon idea positively, not negatively, if possible.

Instead of focusing on the negative consequences of an action or sin, put the focus on what can be done to avoid that sin or how we can please God. There are times the sermon idea is negative, but that should be the exception and not the rule. People will respond to the positive much better than the negative.

4. State it in words or phrases that are precise, concrete, and familiar to your listeners.

It is not wise to use words or terms that you will have to explain. If you have to explain words in your sermon idea, the likelihood of the audience remembering the main idea of your sermon is very minimal.

5. State it so that your audience readily sees the truth as relevant and applicable.

If the audience does not see the sermon idea as relevant, they will not see it as important.

INTERVIEW

WITH

RAYMOND WOODWARD

Below are comments taken from an interview with Raymond Woodward, pastor of Capital Community Church (Fredericton, New Brunswick, Canada), on the importance of developing the sermon idea:

How do you determine the big idea?

The big idea to me is whatever inspires me the most. Because if it lights something up in me, I feel I can get it to light something up in someone else. If it is just purely academic in me, I can try and sometimes it will work. But to me, that is one of your "pre-packaged" Wednesday night Bible Studies that is put together during a busy week. But the church needs to be fed. This is your responsibility and it must be done. In these situations I will either have a thought, something I've been reading, a Scripture that has really grabbed me, or I am going to go back to all those inspired ideas that I have been collecting forever. Then I am just going to settle down and start reading them through. Typically I will read through about three or four of those long miscellaneous notes and something will click. Sometimes it's not even one of those thoughts; but it stirs something else, and that's how I jumpstart if I am dry.

But there I am taking an idea and I am crafting a Bible study. It will be Word. It will be decent, but it is not in the same category of getting this inspired idea that's just "Oh my goodness, let me write this down before I forget it." If I get one of those, that's what I'm building around, and that's what I am crafting towards. That's how I know that this is the moment I am going to try to illuminate. Other than that, I am going to pick what I think is the strongest point.

There is always the exception. There are times when a certain topic needs to be preached. It doesn't matter if it is strong here or there. This is the Word that needs to be taught for this situation and in this moment. I think that reflects maturity in teaching and preaching.

I don't get stressed out over structure. As corny as it may sound, I have this innate confidence in the Word that it will work with me, in spite of me, or independent of me. And if you preach the Word, the Word has its own power. That sounds like something cliché to say, but I have come to that realization after a lot of years of preaching and teaching. I really believe the Word has power.

How do you stay focused in the development of the sermon? What do you think keeps preachers and teachers from staying focused?

I really try to make it my business to read books about preaching. One of those books is *Communicating for a Change* by Andy Stanley. He is a one-thought preacher. I tend to go real broad and deep too, which is a lot like quicksand. Stanley says if a preacher cannot express that sermon in a single sentence they are not ready to preach it.

For young preachers, number one, put it in a single sentence. If you can't, you don't know enough about what you are going to talk about to preach it yet. Secondly, once you have it in a sentence then think through your progression. Think of it as a crescendo. How are you structured so that this sentence comes through with the most force?

A lot of young preachers will start out so hot and so high and then they run out of gas. The part they fail to think about is, what do they want these people to do?

Rick Warren says Scripture is given for four purposes as found in II Timothy 3:16—doctrine, reproof, correction, instruction in righteousness. So every time you look at scripture, you look at doctrine (what to believe), reproof (what not to believe), correction (how not to behave), instruction in righteousness (how to behave). So you are always, in every message, looking for "here's what to believe, what not to believe. Here's how to behave and how not to behave." If you don't have one of those in a message somewhere, then it is just clutter. You are not giving anybody any handles on the Word of God.

You are trying to get the what, the so what, and the now what. That is a message right there. That is the funnel and the crescendo. Forget teaching and preaching style. Everybody has to head in a certain direction so that you max out your opportunity to leave people thinking, "Oh, that's what I do with this." And I think that is where we fall apart with young preachers. People are cheering them on because they want to be kind and they love the Word, but they leave confused because that young preacher never told them what to do with what he or she said.

INTERVIEW

WITH

CLAUDETTE WALKER

Below are comments taken from an interview with Sister Claudette Walker (Troy, Michigan), on the importance of developing the sermon idea:

How do you determine what to focus on in a sermon?

Usually with me, the focus comes first—that seed that is dropped in my heart. It usually:
1. Ministers to me.
I have found if it doesn't minister to me it probably won't be a very good sermon.
2. Intrigues me greatly.

3. It makes me want to dig and study.

That becomes the seed thought of that sermon.

Recently I preached a sermon at our church I had been working on for over a year. Sometimes it will develop in a few days. Sometimes it takes a long time to develop that seed thought.

It is kind of like a seed dropped in my heart. I then start watering it with prayer, fasting, and the Word. I will then let it grow and let it develop. I will also seek the Lord about timing of when to preach it because a message has to be fully matured and developed before it is preached. Sometimes you can preach a message too soon.

How do you stay focused in the development of the sermon?

Someone once said, "Tell them what you are going to say, say it, and then tell them what you said." Though simple, this helps me stay focused. Is this part I want to add really going to enhance what I am trying to say or not? Is it really going to add to this seed God put in my heart? If not, then leave it out.

INTERVIEW

WITH

CHESTER MITCHELL

Below are comments taken from an interview with Chester Mitchell, pastor of Capital Community Church (Ashburn, Virginia), on the importance of developing the sermon idea:

I really try to discipline myself to preach systematically. This is something I learned from W. C. Parkey while serving on the curriculum committee. I watched him and could tell he was a very disciplined thinker.

One thing I do toward the end of the year—I am a simmering type of guy—is start thinking about the next year. I begin thinking, *What is the overall vision, theme, and thrust that I want this church to adapt?* So I start there. "What do I want to say?" When I land on what God wants, I try to be able to say it to you in about one sentence.

I then begin thinking thematically: "What do I want to preach." I will come up with an idea, a thought, and a theme. "What are the four messages I want to preach in January?"

I have a preaching partner. Before I get too far into it, he and I will get in a room and I will tell him, "This is what I am thinking and what I want to preach on. Here are my four points for January." I will just talk it through with him and allow him to help me get the thoughts simmered down into four messages that I will preach.

A lot of preachers struggle because they are not disciplined in their preparation. A lot of them struggle because they have not discovered the benefit of having someone— maybe two or three people—to really help them with their preaching. I think having a team of people helping them with their preaching would increase the effectiveness of their preaching by 30-40 percent.

Why do you think preachers don't do this?

They may be scared. But we are also prisoners of how we were trained. The guy who was in front of you waited until Saturday night for God to speak. So you assume God only speaks on Saturday nights from 11 PM to 1 AM. I have broken away from that. I assume God can speak to me sometime this year about a theme for next year. I assume that by the time I am through December I will know what I am going to be preaching about in January and February. A lot of times guys are stuck in a pattern that was delivered to them.

How do you stay motivated to preach on a regular basis even when you are tired, stressed, or just plain lacking the "want to"?

The principal thing that keeps me driven to excel in the art of preaching (without humanizing this) is the needs of the people and the dependence they have on a touch and a Word from God. Every Sunday there is somebody in the congregation whose eternity could very well depend on what happens that day. In any congregation, there are people who are going to go to Heaven no matter what the preacher does. There are those who will probably be lost no matter what the preacher does. But then there's this group in the middle I can influence, that God through me can influence—that the preaching can have an effect on.

I can't become complacent because of the first group or offended by the ones who never move. They may not move if Jesus Himself showed up to preach. But I can't get distracted by that. There is this bigger segment in the middle and what happens in the service has the potential to shape their lives. I am past the point where I need compliments or someone patting me on the back and saying, "That was fantastic." That doesn't drive me. The thing that compels me is knowing there are people who are hurting. And I've been given the staggering privilege and responsibility to touch their eternity with the Word of God. That drives me. That's what compels me to try and do my best.

I get my eyes off of me. I'm tired. I was up at the hospital all night. I have to try and preach today. I'm weary. Someone poured cold water on me as soon as I arrived to the church because they were upset the plastic flowers didn't get watered. Those kinds of things happen. And I am not superhuman. I am not above getting distracted by that stuff. But the thing that helps me focus is to take my eye off that individual and realize that somewhere out there, someone needs this message today. There are days and times when I thought I did a really good job and it seems no one was affected. Then other times I preach and wonder if I really did a good job. Then I get a note two or three days later from somebody who says, "That was the Word I had to hear that day." That's what drives me. Not the compliment of "you did a good job" but the compliment that says "that was the Word I needed to hear."

When I entered the Youth Division, I had tremendous opportunities to preach at many different churches. At one point, I was visiting with an elder pastor and I asked him a question: "How do you keep it straight? You are well-known. You have everybody and their dog coming up, patting you on the back, telling you how wonderful you are. How do you keep that in focus?" And he told me that when he preaches at some settings, people will come up and pat him on the back and say "That was great!" But I will never forget his response. He said, "When I get back to my motel room or my house, the first thing I do is I get on my knees. My prayer is: 'God, these sweet people of Yours wanted to give You a compliment, but they mistakenly gave it to me. So I've carried them. And I've brought them here to You, to tell You that Your people think You did a really great job tonight.'"

I have tried to do that also after hearing this great elder's advice.

This ties in because I want to keep this focus: "It is not all about me." I heard Johnny James say one time, "There are sermons you hear and the people walk out saying, 'my God, what a preacher.' There's other sermons you hear and you walk out and people are saying, 'my preacher, what a God!'" And that's what I want the focus to be. I must remain focused on the idea that I am pointing people to Him, and bringing Him to them. The thing that keeps me motivated is the people. There is someone out there in the audience, whose eternity could be hanging in the balance. That's what keeps me motivated.

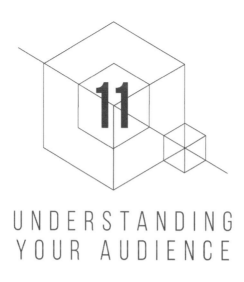

UNDERSTANDING
YOUR AUDIENCE

A little girl was late coming home for supper. Her mother made the expected irate parent's demand to know where she had been. The little girl replied that she had stopped on the way home to help her friend Janie whose bicycle had broken when she fell while riding.

"But you don't know anything about fixing bicycles," her mother responded.

"You are right," the girl said. "But I know Janie. I just stopped to help her cry." (Adapted from *Helping Cry*, by Murray Lancaster.)[33]

Janie needed her bicycle fixed. But what Janie really needed at that moment was someone to share in her sadness—someone to help her cry. Because the little girl knew Janie, she also understood Janie's real need. This allowed her to be the encouragement she needed at that exact moment.

One of the most important elements of sermon preparation is understanding who your audience is. This will present a different level of challenge to those who speak in others' pulpits as opposed to those who have a regularly scheduled date with the same congregation on a weekly basis. However, both preachers have a certain amount of work to do when it comes to matching their message to their audience.

If you are a pastor, you will become familiar with your local congregation's dynamics over time and have a better feel for the people than would an itinerant preacher. Still, it is important for both preachers to understand that every congregation has many of the same dynamics. No public speaker other than a pastor or preacher is ever called upon to speak to such wide emotional needs and maturity levels.

If you were a real estate guru and were called upon to address a conference filled with real estate agents, it wouldn't take long to diagnose that audience. In fact, your choice of topics would probably be quite limited. Every person sitting in that conference came with *very similar needs*. One particular need would most likely stand out: they all want to be better agents. They may have other personal issues; but for those few days, they are there to learn about real estate principles that will help them improve their businesses.

Contrast that to the responsibility of the preacher who stands before an audience on Sunday morning. This audience has come to church with *extremely different needs*. There are grandparents and single twenty-somethings sitting side by side. Across the aisle are six-year-old twin boys who come regularly with their mother, a divorcée. The middle-aged man on the back row just buried his wife, who passed away after a long bout with cancer. Memories of their twenty-eight year marriage floods his mind as he tries to worship. There are fidgety bus kids sitting on the second row, whose parents are still at home in bed suffering from a hangover as a result of the wild party last night. And those are just the people in the left section of the church.

And there you sit in your study, wrestling over the message God has given you for that particular day. How in the world will this one message minister to every one of them? There are so many needs. There is so much brokenness. The thought is overwhelming. There is no way—as far as your human strength and ability goes—for you to answer every question present in the sanctuary this day.

You know you can't—in your own power—help them all. But you are invested in their struggles and have daily taken them to the Lord in prayer. He knows the answer. He is the Answer. And He has placed a message in your spirit. He may have placed it there months ago while you planned in advance. Or he may have woken you up last night and changed your plans. Either way, you have given your audience to the Lord. You don't go into this blindly because you do know many of the situations. Yet you have turned it over to the Lord, who is ultimately in control.

That is the beauty and power of preaching. You may preach a message on giving, and yet most of the people we just referred to will find themselves in the altar, moved, blessed, and encouraged to keep following Jesus Christ.

No doubt, every listener in the congregation has needs. But as a preacher, you are armed with a "Bible full of Band-Aids."[34] There is a balm in Gilead. There is access for them to a Savior, a Healer, and a Deliverer. When you speak words from the Scriptures, those words are life to the spirit and health to the bones. The people have come because they knew there would be hope offered. They are trusting in a God who knows exactly what they need. They are relying on a preacher who has hopefully heard about them from God and has come carrying the answer to their need.

Determining the needs of the audience will be a team effort: you—your deductive ability and common sense—working in tandem with the revelation of the Holy Spirit and the voice of God. You can conclude some things just by watching, thinking, and listening. But the real answers will come as you seek the face of God for His direction and leading.

The impact of the message will depend on two things: the move of the Spirit and how well you—the preacher—have diagnosed your audience. This should not affect your effort in preparation; but if those two elements are in sync, whether or not your content is perfect won't matter. You and God will see eternal things take place.

139

One important element to understand about your audience is "what do they believe?" As our congregations grow, as new churches are planted, and as society changes, we will notice the cookie-cutter congregation is a thing of the past. With a sigh, I say "Thank You, Jesus!" I don't say that because I do not appreciate my heritage, but I say that because it means we are reaching more people, people without Pentecostal roots. What it really means is "revival."

But that being said, this reality means you cannot assume everyone sitting under the sound of your voice believes everything exactly as you were taught. Your congregation is probably composed of a diverse group of believers. They are all at different stages, with different understandings of discipleship, and what it means to have a relationship with Christ.

More and more they come from unchurched backgrounds with little or no understanding of the Bible. It seems paradoxical, but though many of them have not been taught much doctrine, they firmly believe what they believe. In addition, they may not have a lot of convictions but they have an awful lot of opinions.

And the hard part? Convincing them that God should have the last word in their lives . . . on pretty much everything. In this day and age, that sounds ultra-restrictive! They resist authority and the idea of anyone telling them what to do. They don't mind if you express your opinion; just don't make them feel like they have to adopt the same feelings on the subject. Of course, on some things you may express (i.e., personal convictions), they may have a point. But when the Scriptures express a command, we have no grounds upon which we can refuse to comply.

To do this, we first have to lay a foundation of logic and common sense. Appeal to their inner man and the needs within. Settle the idea in your church that we live by the Word of God alone. Show them from Scripture and from real life how we can deceive ourselves. (See I John 1:8.) Tell them that in order to avoid deception, we need a compass, a light, and truth to guide us. Though we cannot trust everything that comes out of Hollywood or the six o'clock news, we can trust a God who is the same yesterday, today, and forever.

You should also consider what they really know about God. In all likelihood, most of them know very little about God. What they do know is probably pretty skewed, because they learned it from Homer Simpson, Oprah, and . . . Tom Hanks. I mentioned him simply because in a 2013 poll, Reader's Digest named him the number one most trusted person in America.[35] I don't know what he has said about God; but if he says anything, people will listen and believe. Why? Because our nation's values are so often tied to celebrity opinions.

The real question is "how can we get them to come to terms with a *requiring God* who sets His agenda somewhat in the mouths of His preachers?" We must come armed, every Sunday, with "Thus saith the Lord." The people need to hear from God. They need to know they are hearing from God. This will only happen when the message is relevant, on target with the audience, and infused with the anointing. In fact, the anointing will break down a lot of barriers.

One such barrier is that many "secular" churchgoers view preaching as being too "preachy." All they see is an opinionated, unmerciful preacher screaming and yelling about how sinful everyone is. We must preach against sin, but realizing who your audience is will help you gain a plan of attack in approaching the subject of sin.

All that being said, we cannot become gun-shy and intimidated by the people we are called to address each and every week. This has happened in many mainline churches. Preachers have become scared to confront sin as they attempt to become *liked* by their audience. I see it as the same complex many parents are struggling with today. Instead of compassionately standing their ground and correcting their daughter because of the inappropriate comments made on social media, they shrug it off as "no big deal" and slide up beside her trying to be her friend. They are afraid of her rejecting them. Sadly, they end up losing her respect because what she really needed was a parent, not a friend. She was looking for boundaries, that's why she stepped where she stepped. It may not seem like it, but everyone wants to know where the line is.

So don't believe all the myths out there. People not only want to know how fine the line is that separates righteousness from unrighteousness, they also want to know how to overcome barriers and touch God. If someone says churches don't want to hear messages about transcendence—that which exists outside the created or known world—it is just not true. People are hungry for the supernatural. They want to hear about Heaven. They want to hear about Hell. They are searching for something beyond them and this present world.

We live in a world filled with zombies, werewolves, and wizards. The inner man knows there is something more than the natural world we see with our eyes. Our spirits are crying out for more. That desire is God-given, and God has the answer to that desire. More than anything we need the supernatural evident in our churches. They may be skeptical at first; but they want to hear about the gifts of the Spirit— why and how they operate.

Others say people don't want to hear sermons on doctrine. Again, this is not true. People want to be taught about the major tenets of God's Word. We need to go back to the basics again and again. They need to hear about God and His oneness. They need to hear about Jesus, as God manifest in flesh. They need to hear about the rapture of the church. They need to hear about salvation, the new birth, and Acts 2:38. They need to hear about the inerrancy of Scripture. And there are other doctrines that should be taught regularly, no matter the audience.

Finally, the audience wants to hear two things:

1. They want to hear and feel like their life has significance.

People want to be told they have been called and chosen for a purpose. (See John 15:16; I Peter 2:9.) They want to know God designed them for a reason before they were even formed in their mother's womb. (See Jeremiah 1:5; Psalm 139:13-14.) They want to know God sees them and has given them unique talents and abilities. (See Romans 12:5-8; I Peter 4:10.) They want to know they are needed and have a reason to keep believing in what they have been taught from God's Word. (See I Corinthians 15:58; Hebrews 4:14.)

2. They want to be instructed how to cope with their pain.

People want to know God has a future for them, even though they may be walking through a valley (Jeremiah 29:11; Philippians 1:6). They want to know that not only will they make it through this struggle, but that they have been made more than conquerors (Romans 8:37; II Corinthians 2:14). They want to know that even though they have made mistakes, they don't have to be defined by those mistakes. God can make them new again (II Corinthians 5:17, I Corinthians 6:11). They want to know there is hope. Really all they need is hope (Romans 8:28; 15:13).

No matter who your audience is . . . give them hope!

What are three things a preacher can begin doing today to improve their preaching?

1. Rediscover and reaffirm your faith in preaching; that preaching is the power of God. That it alone saves. That it's meaningful. It's not an exercise of human ego. It is the choice of God. And the best thing you can do about anything is preach. It doesn't mean you preach about the problem, but when you preach you open up the avenue for the Spirit of God to speak to people's hearts. So reaffirm that preaching works and that it is the highest calling you have. If you denigrate preaching and relegate it to some secondary or tertiary level, you are relegating the power of God in your ministry to a lower level.

2. Recommit to preach the Word of God—that every sermon will be the Word of God. It will be the Bible. That its basis will be the Bible; the heart of it will be the Bible. You don't have to be expository or topical; but the premise of it, the basis of it, and the proof of it is the Bible.

3. Recommit to a genuine relationship with God, fundamental, simple, to walk with God. Recognize we're human, but our strength comes from our walk with God.

We all know these things, but I think in the hectic, demanding pace that we all live, every once in a while, we just need to reconfirm some of these things. Don't be embarrassed to be a preacher. It's going to get worse as time goes on. The world will not relate to us. But it's still the power of God.

PRAYER
AND THE MESSAGE

Talking to men for God is a great thing,
but talking to God for men is greater still.
—E. M. Bounds

We must never get to the point where we do the job of preaching without prayer. In so doing, we make preaching a job and not a calling. Just as true preaching is biblical preaching; true preaching is only accomplished through prayer.

INTERVIEW

CHESTER MITCHELL

Below are comments taken from an interview with Chester Mitchell, pastor of Capital Community Church (Ashburn, Virginia), on the importance of prayer and the message:

My preaching flows out of my devotional life. That is what I saw with Bishop Haney. His preaching flowed out of his devotional life. I was close enough to him to watch him on a daily basis, and I noticed that he preached out of his time with God. Quite often I would see him praying and then stopping to go to his legal pad to write down his thoughts, which became the seed for his sermons.

However, on the other side, there is nothing that can take the place of preparation. You just have to prepare.

What have you learned about prayer and its importance in the life of the preacher?

There are so many voices coming at you; when do you hear that still small voice? When do I hear the still small voice? I don't hear it when I am surfing the web or on Twitter. I hear the still small voice when I get alone with God and listen for His voice to speak. When I get with Him, I hear that still small voice again and again. Later on when I deliver the message, I am always the most surprised guy in the room. I think, "Oh my, what if I had not heard that?"

In my mind, a preacher has to really value and guard the times when he or she can get alone and shut out every voice. Don't worry about what the guy down the road is preaching or what the guy on television is preaching or what the people are saying in your circle of fellowship. What is God saying to you? You are not going to hear that unless you have a devotion time with God.

What does it mean to have a "prayer life"?

I think what it means is that you are sensitive and respectful enough of the ministry that you carve out time where you listen for God and talk with God. I don't think it necessarily has to be a formal thing where you are on your knees for eight hours or two hours. It is sensitivity to the fact that you need to hear God's voice. I have heard the voice of God driving down the road. While I was driving, the need to hear His voice was on my mind; I was in prayer. I have heard it on an airplane while I am sitting there with my legal pad or on my iPad.

What would you say to the preacher who has neglected his life of prayer?

You are really missing out on hearing and knowing what God wants you to do. The longer you preach, you can get to a point in your ministry that if some Sunday you don't want to talk to God about something to speak you can pull something out on your own. It may have been good when you first preached it. But you must never do that unless you sense that is what God wants you to do. I have done this; but if I do, I am going to deliver it in such a way that even if the people recognize it, they are going to see a different passion and anointing because it is a timeless message.

A preacher just really needs to discipline himself to spend time with the Lord. I think we do ourselves a disservice when the great God has something He wants to say but we don't listen.

INTERVIEW

WITH

JOEL URSHAN

Below are comments taken from an interview with Joel Urshan, pastor of First Apostolic Church (Cincinnati, Ohio), on the topic of prayer and the message:

What do you see as the connection between prayer and the message?

"Content comes from study. Passion comes from prayer"— Anthony Mangun. If I will pray and seek God, it really opens the windows of Heaven. Whenever I pray, it doesn't matter what leads me to a particular Scripture, I will go there. This is how I encourage people to study their Bibles. Whatever Scripture comes to mind, whatever name, whatever story emerges in your thinking for whatever reason, go there. Start there. If it is a story you have not read in a while, read that story from when that person was born to when that person died. If it was a passage of Scripture that was meaningful to you as a child and you haven't revisited because you think you know it so well, go back and read it from beginning to end. I make that a part of my prayer.

It has been said if you have time to only pray or only study, always choose prayer. Do you agree?

Jesus said, "The Comforter shall come in my name and He shall bring all things to your remembrance, whatsoever I have said unto you." So when we study, we are obviously gaining new information. But when we pray, we are touching God and hearing the voice of God. To me, the Word of God is simply the voice of God transcribed. When we hear the voice of God it is going to be this Word in vocal form. When you begin to pray, the Word of God will become very pronounced.

INTERVIEW

WITH

CLAUDETTE WALKER

Below are comments taken from an interview with Sister Claudette Walker (Troy, Michigan), on the subject of prayer and the message:

How would you describe the relationship between prayer and the sermon?

I believe they are inseparable. In my personal experience, every sermon I have ever preached or lesson I have ever taught was born out of prayer. It was not born out of my desire to preach a message or teach something. I rarely seek to craft a sermon. I am always seeking just to know God for myself and to obey Him. Anything I have ever had to say publicly is born out of that.

I heard Nona Freeman say once that even after she retired as a missionary and after they had become regional field supervisors for Africa, she would still read through the Bible every year simply for her own personal growth, along with all of her studies for teaching, preaching, and writing books. That impacted me so much as a young woman that I have tried to follow her example. There have been a few years that the Lord has had me on another plan, but most of the time I will seek to read through the Bible every year just to know God and to obey Him. I will also journal on thoughts I have while reading the Word. Almost everything I've ever preached comes out of those journal thoughts—close to

250 pages every year that I journal on my own study of the Word of God.

What do you pray about in regards to the message you will be preaching?

The first thing I pray is probably the obvious: that I will hear God's voice and what He wants to say to the people. The second thing is that the message will be burning brightly in my own life and heart as I preach. Paul said, I'm a living epistle known and read of all men. I heard a quote once: "Who you are speaks so loudly, that I can't hear a word you are saying."

I heard Bill Gothard say that "a message prepared in the mind can reach someone's mind and minister to their intellect for a short time. A message prepared in our emotions can affect people's emotions for a very short time. But a message prepared in a life will teach, touch, and change lives forever."

People are not just listening to a sermon, they are listening to our lives. So it is integral that we become—not just preach the message—whatever it is we are saying.

What have you learned in your ministry about the impor-tance of prayer in the life of the preacher?

I am a very visual learner, and sometimes God will give me a mental image to help me with certain things. Several years ago I was going to speak at a Texas District Ladies' Conference. I was young and kind of intimidated, straining—like we all do at times—to come up with something to say. I was sitting up in bed and could see my bathroom sink. I saw the faucet and the Lord just said to me, "Does that faucet have to strain in order to get the water to flow through it? What does the pipe do?"

I was thinking, *well, I am not a plumber, but I assume it just stays connected to the source. And secondly, the pipe stays cleaned out so the water can flow through it freely.* I felt like the Lord just gave that to me, not just for preaching a sermon, but for my life. I have to construct the pipeline through prayer and stay connected to the Source. Then it comes through and out of me, whether I'm preaching or just living my life and talking to people.

Secondly, I must keep it cleaned out through repentance and fasting. As we worked with J. T. Pugh early on in ministry, I would overhear him in prayer saying often, "None of self, but all of Thee." Because of this, I feel like the anointing will flow whether or not I am preaching a sermon or just living my life. Prayer is the source to that pipeline.

What does it mean to have a prayer life?

I asked my husband about something the Lord spoke to him early on in life. He was in college and was studying on the verse that says, "Pray without ceasing" (II Thessalonians 5:17). He wondered how he could do that. And the Lord spoke to him and said, "Think your thoughts unto me continually." In other words, don't have a private thought life separate from God. The Lord told him that his prayer time is not relegated to thirty minutes in the morning, but that he should be actually seeking to think all his thoughts as unto the Lord and rely on His Spirit. Seek to hear His voice and direction throughout your whole day—whether for big decisions or small decisions. It is almost like having a spiritual GPS installed in your life. The Book of Acts records over and over, "The Spirit forbade me. The Spirit bade me to go. The Spirit said, 'No.'" Paul wanted to go somewhere, and the Spirit said, "No." He obviously had something going on constantly in his thought life with God, where God could easily guide him throughout his day. That is my goal. I can't say I am there yet.

What would you say to a preacher who has neglected their prayer life?

Paul said, "But I keep under my body, and bring it into subjection: lest that by any means, when I have preached to others, I myself should be a castaway" (I Corinthians 9:27). I remind myself of this verse all the time.

I have prayed and meditated on these poems for years:

> I would rather see a sermon than hear one
> any day
> I would rather one would walk with me than
> merely show the way
> For I might misunderstand you and the high
> advice you give
> But there is no misunderstanding in how you
> act and how you live.
> —Edgar A. Guest (*I'd Rather See a Sermon*)

> I have to live with myself and so
> I want to be fit for myself to know . . .
> I don't want to look at myself and know that
> I'm just bluster and bluff and empty show
> —Edgar A. Guest (*Myself*)

Almost every preacher Marv and I have talked to who has failed, if they are honest (as we try to counsel with them), one of the first three things they say is always, "I stopped praying. I really neglected my prayer life."

I asked C. M. Becton once when he came to preach in Cincinnati, how he, when God asks him to preach the same thought or sermon over again, "Do you ever feel guilty preaching something again and again." He said, "I never feel guilty preaching the same thing over again. However, when God asks me to preach the same message again, I will never preach that sermon until I have prayed in such a way that the sermon is born in my own heart once again and is as fresh and fiery in me as it was the first time I preached it."

Who has made the biggest impact on you as a preacher?

My dad was amazing because he took the time with my brother and me. We would sit in the living room and talk at length about preaching and about scripture. No question was off limits. We would talk about everything. We would talk about preachers from the past, their style, messages they were known for. W. E. Gamblin was a great "One-God" preacher. George Glass Sr. preached "Thou hast magnified Thy Word above Thy Name."

My dad also brought a wide variety of preachers into our church. Some operated in the Spirit; some were skilled in praying people through to the Holy Ghost; others were really deep Bible teachers; others were prolific masterpiece preachers who could carve thoughts out of the Bible and turn them into these beautiful messages.

When you talk about the messages that were preached that impacted me, two men really stand out: J. T. Pugh and Bishop James Johnson. J. T. Pugh preached a message when I was a kid, "The Removal of Humiliation." I remember as a kid on the front row mesmerized, just listening. I didn't "amen" one time, and I was a big "amen corner" kind of kid. He preached and I was spellbound. I was impressed with his seamless interweaving of Bible stories, personal experiences, historical facts, and scientific discoveries. When he preached one of his classic messages, it was a masterpiece in the truest sense of the word.

Bishop Johnson was different. He would start out so slow. But he had a cadence I grew to deeply appreciate. It was slow, but methodical and systematic. He would slowly draw you into some kind of cyclonic world of truth he was helping you to understand. About three-quarters of the way through his message, you were up on your feet and looking for a chandelier to swing from. He had a cadence and knew how to drive that point home. Those types of dynamics became very important to me.

Also, Edwin Harper from Huntington, West Virginia. He invited me to preach my first revival. While I was with him, he was very deliberate in talking with me about preaching. I was fifteen, and that was my first full-fledged revival.

SERMON
CONSTRUCTION

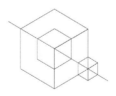

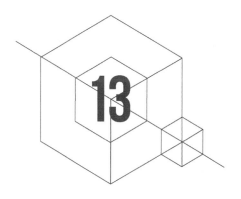

SETTING THE STAGE
WITH YOUR INTRODUCTION

In the early 1980s, Head and Shoulders aired a commercial showing a conversation between two businesswomen. One was about to interview for a new job and became worried about dandruff issues. The other lady encouraged her to use Head and Shoulders because it would help her keep from making the wrong impression during her interview. At the close of the ad, a voiceover relayed this message, "Because you never get a second chance to make a first impression."

Your sermon introduction is that one chance you have at securing the interest of your audience for the next thirty to forty-five minutes. Why should they listen to you? Will they think this is going to be a waste of time? This is your opportunity to show them up front, "I have something to share with you today that will change your life!" You can't simply say that and expect them to listen, but you can craft your introduction in a way they sense that is going to be true.

The introduction is more than just the first part of the sermon. As the congregation prepares to hear truth from God's Word and receive revelation from the Holy Spirit, the introduction gives them a snapshot of where they are headed. It allows them to settle into listening mode and open themselves to the message they are about to hear.

People have a natural aversion to abruptness. It is not profitable for the preacher or the audience if the preacher were to launch from the deep, jumping right into the heart of the message. You will create more questions than answers by doing that. What? How did we get here? What does this mean? The introduction begins their journey from the shore to the deep.

I had a student several years ago who, in his desire to be creative—which I applaud—started his in-class sermon so abruptly, that not only did it leave the class wondering what in the world was going on, it about knocked me right out of my chair.

A classmate introduced him, and this young man quietly approached the pulpit. He gently opened his notes, stared at them for a slight moment and then stepped to the side of the pulpit. There was silence for a good ten seconds, when all of a sudden at the top of his lungs he broke out into a dramatic dialogue about the Cross. The volume startled the class. The dramatic nature of the dialogue was unsettling. And the abruptness of it all threw the entire class off for a few seconds.

We didn't know what to do. Fortunately, he recognized the disruption, pulled back a little and continued. Because it was a class setting, we were all engaged and didn't let the scary intro kill our interest. But if that would have happened in a little country church in Louisiana, he may have had to call an ambulance, or several ambulances, to come take care of the people lying on the ground from heart attacks.

The introduction is supposed to introduce, not overpower. It is supposed to set the stage, not clear it. The initial willingness of the audience to follow a thirty minute exposition has to be piqued. In that quest to pique their interest, somehow you must show them how the upcoming message will address their needs. You won't reveal everything just yet, but it will hopefully prove relevant to them and give them reason to stay tuned.

Not only does the audience need the introduction, the preacher needs it as well. The intro gives the preacher time to bridge that familiarity gap. You won't necessarily want to launch into your complete life's story, but showing your personality and revealing a little about your experiences will go a long way to winning people over. During this time you will also begin testing whether what you observed about the audience during the first part of the service is true or not. Are they ready to receive from God's Word? Are they responsive? Are they engaged and actively listening?

Additionally, the intro gives the preacher an opportunity to dismiss any prejudice in the congregation. From the moment you stepped into the sanctuary and were recognized as the preacher for the evening, the audience members began sizing you up. "He's too young. He's too old." Or maybe even, "He's a she! A woman preacher?" Sadly, this is the truth: many in the congregation have already prejudged you to some degree.

The introduction is your opportunity to put to rest any of those presumptions. Approach the pulpit carefully, but confidently. Begin speaking with surety, knowing you have something important to say. Carry a spirit of humility, not cockiness. Show respect for the audience: their time, their commitment, and their intellect. Let them see by your delivery that you have properly prepared and are ready to give them something that will challenge and change their life.

Anything that does not begin development or set up the sermon is pre-introduction. In most cases, you are allowed some time for this. A few "thank-yous" and an "I'm honored to be here" are appropriate. But once the pre-introduction comments are over, you must launch into the prepared introduction.

The sermon introduction should indicate the purpose of the sermon and establish a good transition to the big idea and body of the sermon. Introductions will take many shapes and forms. In fact, variety at this stage is very important. Try

159

not to become predictable. Don't use the same route every time you develop a sermon.

There are several different sources you could turn to for an introduction:

1. Biblical Context – some preachers enjoy establishing context as a part of the introduction. Sharing background information on the text or the biblical story you will be telling can serve a great purpose in bringing the audience up to speed. However, be careful to not delve too deep into background and context so that the audience is lost in information overload. Remember, you do not have to share everything you have learned in studying for this message. Share only what you need to share. The fact you have put in the background study will come through whether you say it or not. There will be a depth to your delivery others will recognize.

2. Personal Experience – one way to quickly connect with your audience is to relate a personal story or experience that best introduces the topic at hand. Don't preface your personal story by saying, "Forgive me for the personal reference." People enjoy hearing personal references. It shows them you are real and understand what you are talking about. Now if your personal reference is braggadocio or demeaning to others, then you will need to apologize. Or better yet, just choose a different personal reference.

3. Biographical Content – remember, stories about people are more impacting than stories about things. Sharing a situation from someone's life—a famous character from history or present-day—will make the principle or thought you are preaching come to life.

4. Quotations – oftentimes you will find something someone else said captures the idea you are sharing better than you could have articulated it. If that is the case, use the quotation. Sometimes hearing other people say it will bring greater credence. Quotations can even add weight to something said in Scripture. I know we do not treat what others say as being on the same level as Scripture, but hearing it in a different way or from a different perspective may be what that first time guest needed to hear.

5. News Item – is there something going on in the world that would help introduce the topic at hand? Depending on your subject, relating something from the local, national, or world scene can help secure interest quite quickly. If it is a huge news item, they are probably already thinking about it or have thought about it recently. The audience will become engaged when they hear you discuss it at the beginning of your message.

6. Humorous incidents – some use humor quite well because it comes very easily. Others struggle to be funny. If humor is not your forte, then use it sparingly. However, humor can secure interest better than most things. I do have a caution for you: make sure the humor is relevant to the message and that you never disrespect the audience by poking fun at people, cultures, or authorities. Restrain from poking fun at your family too.

Good introductions will arouse the interest of the listener by beginning where they are and then leading them in a direction of God's revealed truth. Thus your introduction needs to be relevant to both the person listening and the text you are going to preach from.

Good introductions will introduce the text and subject of the sermon. They also show how the subject and text connect. Therefore be sure to include your propositional statement, or the sermon's big idea, in your introduction. Be clear, relevant, and well-prepared. It may be beneficial to know your introduction so well enough it can be delivered from memory.

Good introductions should also fit in the 10-80-10 rule for the proportion of your sermon: 10 percent for the introduction, 80 percent for the body, and 10 percent for the conclusion. In a thirty minute sermon your introduction should be no longer than three to four minutes.

INTERVIEW

KEN GURLEY

Below are comments taken from an interview with Ken Gurley, pastor of the First Church of Pearland (Pearland, Texas), on the topic of sermon introductions:

How long should an intro be?

I feel the introduction is a "tithe" of the message: 10 percent of the total. Any less and it indicates a lack of clarity; any more and it indicates a lack of substance.

Do you write your intro or conclusion first? Why?

I write the introduction first.

In the early research phase, I let my mind wander and accumulate anything and everything I can think of that may be of use in the message. However, in the actual preparation phase, I start with the introduction and move in order through the message to the conclusion. I find that it keeps the points straight and clear in my mind.

Do you prefer writing your intro out word for word?

Yes. I've always done this. Writing out an illustration word for word permits me to polish the words and to make certain I'm sharing only as many words and concepts as necessary prior to the body of the message.

Do you find yourself using a certain style of intro or perhaps using some template for your intro?

Variety is indeed the spice of life, and a varied approach in opening illustrations yields a greater opportunity to be heard. I will, at times, begin with a humorous story, a personal illustration, or something that I read.

In your mind, what is the goal of an introduction?

More often than not, I'm looking for an opening story that will transition the audience from where they are in life and in the service itself to where they need to go.

What does an effective intro do?

An effective introduction is "the hook" that captures the imagination, makes relevant the subject matter, and provides the audience an opportunity to book passage on the coming journey.

Do you give the main point (focus) in the intro or simply allude to it?

I generally allude to the main point without putting a fine line on it.

Does it introduce your subject (like we were taught writing papers in English), or does it introduce the "mood" while tying it to the subject in some way?

An effective introduction establishes mood first and communicates the approach to be taken to discuss a particular subject even before the subject itself is revealed. To me, the introduction brings the audience to the edge of the subject matter and the Scripture text introduces the subject.

With your intro, do you like to create intrigue or spark questions?

Some ministers will use the introduction to provoke the audience's sensibilities by making controversial statements or provoking questions. I am more concerned with capturing interest than sparking questions.

INTERVIEW

WITH

WAYNE HUNTLEY

Below are comments taken from an interview with Wayne Huntley, pastor of The Temple of Pentecost (Raleigh, North Carolina), on the topic of sermon introductions:

Do you write the intro or conclusion first?

I write the intro out. For me, the hardest part of preaching is to get the message. What is the message?

How long should an intro be? What portion of the message should it take up?

The introduction is predicated on a title. I am a very title-conscious person. A message without a title, to me, is a message that will not be remembered. A lot of times all they remember is the title. A title puts a handle on the sermon so people can get a grip on what you are saying. Because of the title, they will also have something to carry out of the service. Most Pentecostal assemblies have been trained to appreciate titles. It grabs them in that moment. It creates some intrigue. So whenever I am doing an introduction, I like my introduction to be filled with intrigue. I like to take the negative and make it positive.

It is my experience that when you come to the pulpit and preach, you have just a matter of a couple minutes where the audience decides whether they are going to receive you or not; whether they are going to help you or not. Now a lot goes into that: your posture on the platform, your involvement in the first part of the service, even the way you walk to the pulpit when you are introduced. Your first response and your first few words determine the mind of the audience—if you are worthy of their attention.

What I try to do is to say something that will appeal to their mind and tease their intellect. You must appeal to the mind to tease the intellect. You appeal to their spirit to ignite their spirit. But of course the real target of preaching is the heart. The introduction should, in some small segmented way, touch all those areas to get a good hold on that audience right from the beginning.

I like to measure and weigh every word, because the audience cannot absorb but so many words. Your words should be pointed. They should be weighed. They should be highly selected, because you can't waste words.

The message is a vehicle. When you start preaching, you want to put people into that sermon. The message is like a vehicle to move them from point A to point B. It is all about taking them from where they are to where you have been in the Spirit: the place you know God wants them to go in that service. That's what the message is about. It is to capture them, put them in that vehicle with you, take them from doubt to faith, from weakness to strength, from sickness to healing, from confusion to peace, or wherever it is God is leading you to take that particular audience on that day. That is the vehicle of the message.

What are three things a preacher can begin today to improve their preaching?

1. They should choose to be more systematic and less sporadic about their preaching. We are not doing ourselves a favor if we are of the order that God only speaks to us late on Saturday night. That is just an excuse for not preparing.

2. I think we need to be aware of not just what we say but how we say it. We are speaking to a post Judeo-Christian audience. Just putting truth out there is not going to work. They don't even believe the Book you are preaching from. You must come to them from a much more relational perspective. Before you give them the truth, give them you. You are the message. If they can't get past you, your message is sunk. If they don't believe you, they don't believe your message. We have to respect the people we are talking to. We can't talk down to them. We cannot assume they have the foundational truths we know and build on. They don't have that at all. So we have to come a different route.

3. Our sermons have to be very practical. We need to be preaching more "How to" messages. Give practical steps to help people. The world is starving for guidance. Sermons should not be up there, pie in the sky stuff where the person sitting there doesn't walk out and know what to do. Especially men—men want to know, "What is my next step?"

STRUCTURING YOUR MESSAGE FOR GREATEST IMPACT

In its most basic form, every story has a beginning, a middle, and an end. The beginning will give us the setting, introduce some of the main characters, and will most likely unveil a situation that produces some kind of conflict in the main character's life. The middle will then delve deeper into this "situation" filled with conflict, complications, obstacles, and some kind of crisis. The end will bring everything to a climax, and finally, to some sort of resolution that hopefully leaves the individuals watching or reading the story pleased with the outcome.

The setting, characters, tension, conflict, crisis, and climax all work together to make the story interesting and exciting. However, the art of writing a good story does not come easy. We have all taken a shot at telling a bedtime story and you may be pretty good at it. But the best storytellers know how to take each of these elements and put them together in such a way that the audience—even if it is your nine-year-old daughter—listens intently, hanging on every word.

It is not enough knowing the elements of a good story. Knowing how to fit them all together is what turns good storytellers into great storytellers.

Conversely, it is important to know the elements of a good sermon. But knowing how to fit them all together is what turns good preachers into great preachers.

Just like a story, in its most basic form, a sermon will have a beginning, middle, and end. The elements placed within these particular stages are crucial to the sermon's impact.

The introduction (chapter 13) sets the direction and gives the audience an understanding of what is coming up.

The sermon idea, or propositional statement, (chapter 10) is a clear, concise statement which describes the central idea of the sermon.

The main points (chapter 15) provide the structure for the sermon. These points will all support the sermon idea and continue to move the sermon along to its intended conclusion.

Transitions are brief, planned statements between the main points to help provide unity between thoughts, and cohesiveness to the sermon.

An illustration (chapter 16) is often a story or analogy used to clarify a point or thought, making it easier for the listener to remember the point.

A conclusion (chapter 17) will sum up the sermon, give finality to the overall theme, and help the audience know what to do in response to what they have heard.

The introduction, sermon idea, main points, transitions, illustrations, and conclusion all work together to make an impact on its intended audience. However, just like a story, the art of creating a good sermon does not come easy. We have all heard great sermons. We can all point out great sermons when we hear them. As our own worst critic, we probably feel like most of the sermons we have preached were not that great. The truth is, we all have room for improvement.

INTERVIEW

WITH

JERRY JONES

Below are comments taken from an interview with Jerry Jones, general secretary of the United Pentecostal Church International, on the topic of structuring a sermon for greatest impact:

What is your philosophy in structuring a message?

The overall picture I keep in my mind when I'm working on a sermon is what the end result of every sermon is: to elicit a response—to get people to do something. When you keep this firmly in mind, it moves you toward that moment when you ask the audience to respond.

What that does for me is that it helps me see the points, not as informational but as emotional. And that helps me gauge what the ending point will be and what will bring me to that moment where people will say, "I want to respond."

Then, in my mind—and I don't know that I would recommend this to a young preacher starting out—I work backward from there. Once again, I already know the flow of the sermon, in the sense that I know what I'm going to preach. I have my points. Everything's laid out there. But I want to get to that final point, so I work backward from that point.

I understand that I have to draw the audience in. So my second most powerful idea needs to be in my introduction, or introduced as my first point. Then I have the luxury between the beginning point and the ending point (the call to action), where I can educate, teach, even challenge.

You can't hit a good high point to draw people in and then bottom out and stay on the bottom. It doesn't work like that. On the other hand, you can't make a good point to draw them in and then hit the top and stay at the top. You'll lose them either way. There has to be a rhythm. There has to be a cadence.

This is the great challenge of the actual preparation of the sermon: keeping in mind that the goal is not to impress anybody, educate anybody, or teach anybody. Those things happen, but they are not the goal. The goal is to get a response; an emotional and logical, but mainly an emotional response. And that's where you learn to gauge the various points and their impact on the crowd.

What are the most important elements of the sermon?

First is *the Bible.* We need to preach the Bible. It's easy not to preach the Bible and think we are because we are echoing some fundamental principles or teachings that are in the Bible. We need to remind ourselves that we are called to preach the Word of God, the Bible. It should always be the foundation.

Secondly, are *illustrations.* The old adage says, "They (illustrations) are the windows of your sermon." They let the light in. I think every sermon should have a fundamental Bible story. I understand that sometimes you are preaching concepts or principles and you are not preaching *the* story, but there are always Bible stories that will illustrate Biblical principles. It may be something Jesus did. It may be something that happened to Paul. It may be something in David's life, Abraham's life, or Moses' teachings. There's always a Bible window, an illustration. And I think we search until we get that.

Thirdly, of course, is *emotion*—the preacher's emotion and the reaction of the crowd. Again, I'm always puzzled when a preacher says, "I don't preach for reaction." Well, why do you preach then? The whole idea of preaching is a reaction. Even

Aristotle said that's one of the three criteria for successful persuasive speaking.

So, emotion from the pulpit—passion—is important. It doesn't have to be loud, screaming, and jumping, although there's nothing wrong with those things. I mean, we're not the only ones who understand the power of passion. History's greatest speakers—even if they didn't pace the platform—understood the power of voice modulation, voice volume, and how to drive points home with body language. That is a vital part of every sermon. Those three things must be found: The Word of God, good solid illustrations (both Biblical and modern), and emotion (passion). Those things elevate every sermon and they are vital.

All preaching, whether expository or topical, ought to be persuasive.

"Knowing therefore the terror of the Lord, we persuade men" (II Corinthians 5:11). The end result of every sermon should be a response from the crowd. If you don't go for that, then you are not preaching. I don't mean you are bad, you may be teaching, you may even be expounding, but preaching is persuasive. Preaching is proclaiming a truth that alters human experience and life. It is the good news that we preach. That's why the Scripture says that "it pleased God by the foolishness of preaching to save them that believe" (I Corinthians 1:21). Whether it is the initial saving by repenting, being baptized, receiving the Holy Spirit, or whether it's the tune-ups and the constant desire of being renewed and reinvigorated, the saving is a reaction, and it requires the response of the hearer for there to be a supernatural occurrence.

What is an ideal sermon length?

Sermon length is gauged by the success of the sermon in eliciting a response from the crowd. The problem is you don't know if you have gone too long until you already have. There's no way to gauge that. A bad sermon is too long at ten minutes. A good sermon can go an hour and still be effective. I would say, from a practical viewpoint, we live in an era where every preacher should plan to be into the appeal around 35-40 minutes and be pretty much into the altar service around 45-50 minutes. If you're much longer than that it better be an outstanding sermon or you won't get the response.

People are sort of geared to a thirty minute type thing. If you're a younger preacher starting out, my rule of thumb would be 30-40 minutes max. You should be in your altar appeal beginning at 30-40 minutes. Of course, you have to leave room for the Holy Ghost. Sometimes God will inspire you, and things will come to you that weren't in the notes. But if you do "scare up a rabbit," you better leave a rabbit trail off somewhere down the road.

INTERVIEW

SCOTT GRAHAM

Below are comments taken from an interview with Scott Graham, District Superintendent of the Missouri District and Pastor of The Sanctuary (Hazelwood, Missouri), on the topic of structuring a sermon for greatest impact:

How do you structure a message?

When I was in junior high, everybody took speech class. The lady there taught us: introduction, body, and conclusion. And she was very adamant about that. Each element had to be clearly recognizable. The one thing she pounded in us was that your introduction should be shaped like a funnel. It starts broad and then comes to a point. That point is the one thing you want everybody to go away remembering. It is your thesis statement, so to speak. It is the central essence of what you want to communicate. When your speech is done and people are filing out of the room, if you ask them on the way out of the door, "What did he speak about," their synopsis should as closely as possible mirror that one sentence at the end of your introduction.

I am pretty structured in terms of an introduction leading to a central point. This is the core of what I want to communicate. And then, in the body of the message, I explain, expound, reinforce, reiterate, and develop that point. Then the conclusion (closing). But all in all, one set of my notes is probably a lot like the others.

What are the most important elements every sermon must have?

The central point, or thesis statement, is the core nugget. I am frustrated sometimes when I go back after the fact and ask, "if somebody had to come up with one central synopsis, could they do it?" Sometimes I think "yes," and sometimes I think I was a little broad. That one central nugget of truth is important to me. Now it may be fleshed out, and there may be ancillary little things thrown in there; but in essence I want there to be one concise point.

Beyond that, in terms of key elements, I always want to have solid scriptural foundation for that point. I will typically also try to go to other passages of Scripture that reinforce or support that point. I am also big on some kind of illustrative materials. It is not mandated. You can preach, and certainly a great message can be crafted without it. But some kind of illustrative story, anecdote, or historical reference is a lens through which the point becomes clearer. It is not the message, but illustrations can help make the message pop and come to life.

In the conclusion, there must be some kind of synopsis to bring it back to and reiterate the main point. The old advice still makes sense: "Tell them what you are going to tell them, tell them, and then tell them what you just told them."

Finally, there's the application. Communicating truth is great, but what do they do with this now? What am I asking of them? What's the Spirit of God calling them to? Other than just the accumulation of knowledge which has value, what is the application in that conclusion, or at least leading up to the close of the message? Here's how this needs to affect me. This is the prayer I need to pray. This is what I need to do differently tomorrow.

What is an ideal sermon length?

Sermon length varies greatly depending on your target audience and whether you are preaching evangelistically or if you are preaching exhortation to the church. If I am preaching on a Sunday morning to the unchurched, 25 minutes on the top end is my goal. I want to be concise, simple, and straightforward. We will go longer than that on an average Sunday night to the church, 45-50 minutes.

One of the reasons I share with young preachers for not going longer than 20-25 minutes for the average sinner is because they have been programmed by sitcoms. I read that the average sitcom is around 22 minutes after commercials are removed. That is the attention span of the American public. So when you are talking about an unchurched person, they may be fascinated by the show; they have never heard anybody sweat and scream and holler, so they are intrigued. But their attention span is very limited. That's why I shoot for 20-25 minutes for an evangelistic message on Sunday morning, and a 45 minute target on Sunday night to the church.

How many points should a sermon have?

I would say every sermon needs just one central point. It may have branches to it. It may have different applications, and it may get made repeatedly. But I don't want the congregation walking out after service; and when asked what the preacher preached about, they say, "This and this and this."

I have always wanted to do this, but my ego would probably be slaughtered. I would love to hand out a piece of paper after service to people and ask them, "In one sentence, summarize what he just preached." Of course, this would not be perfect because the wonder of the preached Word is that people hear things according to where they are. But how close would they come to what I think I said? Communication is the art of what is heard, not what is said. Did they hear what I think I said, or did they hear something different?

Preaching is an art. The structure of your sermon will make a huge difference in determining how long people listen to what you are saying and how well they will understand what you said.

What is the most important part of the sermon?

The *second* most important part is just getting people's attention. I teach the young ministers of my church, "In the first thirty seconds you have to give people a reason to listen to you. Don't assume that just because you are behind the pulpit that people are just going to want to listen to you. You better give them a reason to listen to you for the next thirty minutes."

The most important part is the closing. There are a lot of ways to close a message. But what is the point of the message if you don't close it and demand action on the audience? We don't preach in a sterile vacuum. Preaching is a flowing, living, dynamic experience. I don't ever close a message without giving an altar call. To me that is the most important thing. You are giving them an opportunity to respond to God which is the whole point of preaching. Our goal is to help people's hearts get to a place where they will respond to the Lord.

CREATIVITY

INTERVIEW

WITH

T. F. TENNEY

Below are comments taken from an interview with T. F. Tenney, former Louisiana District superintendent, on the topic of creativity in the sermon:

When it comes to making memorable points, what is your philosophy?

It has to be relevant. Jesus was relevant. He used soil, crops, and sores. That was relevant language. He used fishing because that was relevant language. Today He might use computers and other terms that would be germane to our situation. If you want something to be memorable, it has to be relevant. There is an old saying that says, "so many times preachers scratch people where they aren't itching." I have to be careful to remember what was relevant in my generation may not be relevant today.

How do you stay focused on the main purpose of the message, when crafting several points in a sermon?

First of all, it must be Christocentric, or Christ-centered. The bottom line should be, "Does it glorify Him?" If that is not the focus of the whole thing, then you will miss your mark. For instance, in a tapestry there are many different colors and threads; but when the tapestry is completed, you don't say, "That is a beautiful thread." You say, "That is a beautiful tapestry." There are a lot of threads that go in different directions. But what does the finished product say? When you get through, do they see one piece of fabric? I have heard a lot of preachers, and I would sometimes say, "Where in the world is he going?" But when he got through, I saw it. If he would've stopped where I asked the question, it would not have made sense. But when I heard him all the way through, I saw the whole fabric.

How many main points does a sermon need?

They used to say, you must have an opening, a body with at least three points, and a conclusion. But you don't dictate to the wind. You put up a weathervane or a windmill to cooperate with the wind, but you don't dictate to it. The Bible said "the Spirit blows where it wants to blow" (See John 3:8.) You don't dictate to the wind or to the Holy Spirit.

If you are preaching to a large crowd, there are so many needs, you can't address everything. When you get into the message and begin preaching, you have to know when to move from "structure to Spirit." The Spirit may lead you into something beyond your structure. Or it may prompt you to leave your structure. That is the difference in the Spirit-filled ministry. Anything else is little more than a structured lecture.

INTERVIEW

WITH

TOM FOSTER

Below are comments taken from an interview with Tom Foster, pastor of Dallas First Church (Dallas, Texas), the topic of creating memorable main points:

What role do you see creativity playing in the sermon?

Creativity goes back to who you are as a preacher. How creative are you? Are you just reading, listening, looking, and repeating ideas like a parrot? Or are you creative in the development of your ideas? Are you creative in looking and finding that story and illustration?

When you look at creativity as it relates to the sermon, it is important to know who you are preaching to and where you are preaching. You must also try to be creative so that you do not present the same old thing the same old way. I have preached at the same church for over thirty years. There are a few people who have been there the entire thirty years. Even if you have been someplace for only a year; if you are preaching to some of the same people, you have to become creative.

This past Sunday, I preached "Kick the Bucket." You hear people talk about bucket lists. In life, we all have buckets. I placed four buckets on the platform before I began preaching. Two of them contained water. During the message, I kept referring to the buckets:

"Because as you dip out of your bucket and pour into somebody else's bucket, your bucket is still getting full. I can't explain it. I don't know how that happens . . ."

For the most part, the congregation was quiet and intently listening. I made two or three more points and then came to the high point at the very end about "kicking the bucket." We know what that phrase means; it means we die.

I said, "When you die, you want to make a big splash. Because when you are dead, you have to keep living. George Washington, Abraham Lincoln, Martin Luther King, Jr., the apostle Paul, the apostle Peter . . . look at David, Moses, look at Jesus Christ. After they had died, some of their greatest works were done."

So I came up and kicked one of those buckets. Man, water went everywhere. The bucket went crashing, and the audience came unglued. I said, "When I'm dead, I want to be living on. I want my kids, my grandkids . . . I want those I have influenced to the third and fourth generation . . . I want them remembering who I was, what I did, and the impact I had on their life."

And then I kicked the second bucket filled with water. By now they are going crazy. I had the other two buckets. I picked one up and acted like it was real full. All I had in it was really small pieces of confetti. I acted like I was going to throw water on them and when I threw that confetti they went wild. By the time I got to that second bucket filled with confetti, it was over. But it was all about being creative.

Sometimes I use props, sometimes I don't. But you can use words, gestures, people, ideas, poetry, voice inflections, tone—it's all creativity. It is crucial to try not to present the same thing in the same way, where the audience feels like you're a parrot pecking over the same pan of seeds.

What does a preacher need to do to preach a sermon the audience can follow?

It all comes back to preparation and study. You can liken it to the captain of a ship who has to chart his course to be able to reach where he is going. A pilot has to file a flight plan. If you were going to drive from Dallas to St Louis, you would have a map. A message is in many ways the same.

There will be rabbits that will jump up and run while you're preaching. And it is going to be tempting to chase them all over the place. Any little thing can cause you to look this way and that. Maybe some distraction, somebody looking at you wrong . . . somebody sleeping. But I have found if I will stay true to my purpose, have my illustrations and points all lined out, then I am comfortable. But you have to carry the audience along with you.

Preaching is nothing more than storytelling. If you can tell a good story you are going to hold their attention. Looking into their eyes can also be a way to help capture their attention. But you don't want to look too long. If you look too long, then they kind of break off from what you are saying, look away, and get a little embarrassed. They change their train of thought. Then you have to bring them back in again. That is why you can't look at just one person or one area. You can't just preach to half of the church. Look at all the people. That will bring them along with you. Tell them the story and treat it like dialogue.

How do you stay motivated to preach on a regular basis even when you are tired, stressed, or just plain lacking the "want to"?

It all goes back to vision. It all goes back to the dream. It all goes back to that potential you feel. I have been here in Dallas for over thirty years, but I am just like I was when I came here. I know a whole lot more, but that vision, that push, that dream . . . that's why I was up at 5:30 this morning. I'm like, "Let's go!" I spent several hours yesterday with the staff, dreaming, looking at the past, the present, and the future. To stay motivated to preach, it's that vision and it's that potential. I haven't reached it yet. We have to keep reminding ourselves that we must be better. I can't settle. Every Sunday counts. Every day counts.

SELECTING
EFFECTIVE ILLUSTRATIONS

There was one thing about preaching that captivated me as a child. I remember eagerly awaiting the story or interesting illustration I knew would pop up at some point in the sermon. Oftentimes the premise of the message was completely over my head. There were terms I didn't quite understand. There were theological statements made beyond my maturity level. But I could understand the story, and the illustration was something that grabbed my attention.

For a message to be effective, you need to include more than theological statements and well-crafted big ideas. Every sermon needs stories and illustrations.

Dr. Ben Awbrey, professor of preaching at Midwestern Baptist Theological Seminary, gives us two reasons for illustrations in his article "Illustrations."[36]

The first reason they are necessary is because people need them. No matter how well you word your argument or main point, not everyone is going to clearly see it the way you do. However, with the use of an effective illustration, the point can come to life for the individual in the audience. Jesus taught in parables for this very reason.

People still need the assistance of the Spirit to clearly understand spiritual things—Jesus made this clear in Mathew 13:10-18—but spiritual principles are understood more clearly when they are illustrated. Our minds connect with stories much easier than they do with abstract principles.

Secondly, not only do people need illustrations, but truth needs to be illustrated. It is not hearing the truth that sets us free; it is knowing the truth. You cannot know anything you do not understand. For truth to be understood, it will most likely need to be communicated through the use of illustrations, at least to some degree.

Illustrations can serve several functions in a message. For one, they can be used to make abstract truth concrete. They help pull the lofty idea out of the clouds to where it can be clearly understood by those who are listening.

Illustrations can be used to make truth interesting. There were many things in school we didn't care about learning. For some, math was excruciatingly boring. For others, history was dead and lifeless. However, depending on the teacher, both subjects can be exciting. The history professor who knows how to make the American Revolution come to life may inspire lifelong history buffs. The math professor who knows how to give numbers personality through creative methods may find students who go on to pursue math-intensive jobs.

Illustrations can be used to make truth persuasive. It is one thing to hear a preacher tell of the importance of our salvation; it is quite another for a preacher to close his message with a story about someone who wasted their life and never found a place of repentance. The gut-wrenching reality of the illustration has the power—with the help of the anointing—to pull the unresponsive to an altar of consecration.

Illustrations can be used to make truth memorable. I remember the first time I saw someone preaching with a "mantle" draped over his shoulder as he told the story of Elijah and Elisha. Watching the preacher pace the platform—with what was really a blanket from his house lying over his shoulder and down his back—I was caught up in this idea of a physical representation of the anointing and calling of God. I was moved by the understanding that I carry with me something others will likely see, distinguishing me as a man called by God. I was powerfully impacted by what I saw that day. I cannot tell you much of what the preacher said, but the image and the truth that image represented has stayed with me to this very day.

Illustrations can be used to smoothly transition from one point to the next. Good sermons will have rhythm. Well-delivered sermons will have highs and lows, starts and stops. However, for those necessary highs and lows and starts and stops to keep from being distracting, smooth transitions are imperative. Illustrations will serve that role, more often than not, better than anything else.

An effective illustration must serve a purpose. Illustrations are not meant to be stand-alone parts of a sermon. They should connect things and shed light on an idea or main point. Additionally, they must be understandable. The preacher shouldn't have to spend time explaining an illustration. The illustration should be the explanation.

Great illustrations will be about people rather than things. A sermon can quickly lose its punch if it is doused with an illustration that is not relatable. It is much easier for us to relate to people than things. Also, it is much better to use a story rather than an image. PowerPoint images can be effective. But if you can paint a picture in their minds—one with characters, conflict, resolution, and filled with emotional appeal—you will find much more heart response in the hearers.

A great illustration needs both emotional appeal and logical appeal. In other words, it should appeal to both the heart and the head. On one level, it should make an appeal that says, "This idea makes sense, right?" On the other hand, even if the truth is hard to understand—like making a decision to sacrifice something for the kingdom of God—the illustration should reach for the heart and encourage the audience to surrender their lives to the Lord.

185

A great illustration is one that is true rather than hypothetical. A "what if" illustration or story can be effective at times, and sometimes that is all we have; but a true story will almost always make a bigger impact on those in the audience. A true story will hit home when people realize "this is actually possible."

Finally, a great illustration will be developed rather than alluded to. Resist the urge to rush through an illustration or story. Your audience is not as familiar with it as you are. So when it lacks details it may lack impact. The same goes for biblical stories or life stories you assume your audience is familiar with. It is still important for you to take time to develop that story and walk them through it. Maybe they forgot some details, or maybe simply hearing it in the context of your message will cause them to see everything differently.

INTERVIEW

WITH

SCOTT GRAHAM

Below are comments taken from an interview with Scott Graham, district superintendent of the Missouri District and pastor of The Sanctuary (Hazelwood, Missouri), on the topic of effective illustrations:

How do you choose the right illustration?

I don't know if I always do. You know, you find this great story but it doesn't fit what you are preaching. But you get so anxious to use it and you force the issue—you compel it to fit. This does two things: it weakens the message you are preaching, and then it destroys a potential tool you could use later for real value. That is why I try to keep a running file. If I find an illustration that just fits a particular thought,

I will type it in a file and discipline myself not to use it until the right time.

So how do you get the right one? You have patience enough not to use the wrong one. You must realize that you are going to preach again if the Lord tarries. And if He doesn't, we won't care anyway. So if you have found this great story about some war hero in the Battle of the Bulge that made some great statement and it is going to fit really well in a message on faith or faithfulness, well don't force the issue just because it is a great story and decide to use it in your next message on tithing.

Finding the right illustration is probably like finding the right pair of shoes. You start by looking at five hundred pairs you are not going to wear. You would never walk into a store and expect them to have one pair of shoes and make it fit because it is the only pair they have. So if you have only found one illustration and you haven't dug and worked to find a great pool from which to draw, then you are forced to take that one pair of shoes that didn't fit. So the more you have to begin with, the more your chances increase of finding the right one.

Where do you find your illustrations?

There are obviously online resources and sites for sermon illustrations. But some of them are really hokey. I have had people ask me, "That was a great story. Where did you find that?" All I know to tell people is that you have to read and you have to read a bunch. I read a lot. I realize some preachers could have a different philosophy than I do, and I respect that. Some preachers don't read anything that is not church growth or that doesn't come from a Christian bookstore. I can respect that. But some of the greatest illustrations are going to come from biographies. *Reader's Digest* is a great resource. In this one little magazine, you have such broad areas of writing from health to sports, and beyond. When you read, you have to read with this idea: "I'm looking for something I can use." And you have to read from a wide spectrum: biographies, historical accounts, novels, and things on sporting events.

When the Olympics come around, there are a host of materials made available because news reporters are always doing human interest stories on the athletes. When you read news stories online, you are learning certain details about present tragedies in the world. But make sure you watch for the story of the volunteer firemen that ran in without reserve. Read the human interest follow-up stories about those who were affected. You never know when you will find a nugget or statement that was made that will really have an impact on your congregation.

How do you introduce or set up the illustration in your message? And what is your philosophy of delivering the illustration?

Physically, I am prone to move and step away from the pulpit because I'm not as dependent upon my notes at the moment. There is this physical movement that attracts attention. There is probably a change in my tone of voice, maybe even in my countenance. It's a more relaxed moment—"Let me tell you a story"—Now I am not going to say that, but that's what I want to communicate. I want the feeling of: "Hey listen to this. This is pretty cool."

Allan Oggs used to have this phrase he used in his homiletics seminars about "back-dooring a story." By that he meant, one would jump into the story by using a line that the audience wouldn't know what was being talked about. For example, if I were preaching a Wednesday night Bible study about God "chastising those He loves," and I was going to tell this story about a time I got in trouble as a kid and dad had to exercise discipline, I might start the story with, "You know one time when I was six years old . . ." Now you can do that. It doesn't really hurt anything.

But instead of starting with that line, Brother Oggs might suggest starting like this: "I didn't think he could jump that high. I mean, I really didn't." Well, nobody in the audience knows what you are talking about. They don't know who "he" is. Why did you suddenly start talking about "jumping"? Who? What? And you have grabbed them and their attention. "I just didn't think he could jump that high. We had done it before and he had never jumped that high. But on that day my cousin John managed to set a new record in the vertical leap. And you know that ceiling fan that was overhead . . .?" And you have grabbed people.

I love to do that; to backdoor the story. You bring the illustration in by almost jumping in the middle of the story, throwing a line out that causes everybody to have whiplash, "What is he talking about?" Then you flesh it out backwards.

"He did it though. He jumped up and I couldn't believe it. And you know when your head hits a ceiling fan, it doesn't even have to be on high. Because even on medium, really disastrous things happen. And it can be heard all through the house. And I know this, because when I was six years old . . ." And then you tell the story. This is just an effective way of grabbing people's attention.

How do you know if a story or illustration is going to work or not?

There is a danger in something being so cute that it overrides the point. They could remember the story but not the application. Instead of supporting your point, the story could overshadow it. I was talking about Noah one time at Men's Conference. I used this line about the greatest advice God gave Noah was to keep the woodpeckers above the water line. It got a lot of laughs. But that was all they remembered. After service, there were fifteen guys talking about this woodpecker. They were tweeting out pictures of woodpeckers. They were sending each other quotes about woodpeckers. But nobody remembered the point that was being made at the time. There is a danger in that. But I don't know that you really know until you try it. I think you get better at it as time goes by.

There is nothing worse than telling a story—getting two-thirds of the way through it—and realizing you have no idea what point you were about to make out of it. All you have done is tell a great story that has no point. You will get better at it. But to know for sure, you just have to try it. There are no guarantees.

It will vary a lot also. A story that works really well in Mobile, Alabama, may not work in Hartford, Connecticut. You have to be culturally sensitive. It may not be that the story cannot be told, but you have to tell it differently.

I don't remember the exact illustration, but it has something to do with snow. I just remember being in San Diego and preaching and starting to make reference to this thing of shoveling snow. And it dawned on me as I was looking at my notes that afternoon, there's not a human being here, unless they moved here, that's ever shoveled snow. It's a foreign concept to them. I still told the story. I just did it differently.

I remember getting up and saying, "There's this white stuff that falls out of the sky, back in other parts of the country, where they don't have seventy degree weather year round . . ." I kind of razzed them a little about their perfect weather. I used that as the introduction to tell the story. "I realize all you poor spoiled people out here that are suffering . . ." I did that kind of thing and had a little fun with them. "But the rest of us, who live in the 'real' world, have this white stuff that falls out of the sky every now and then, principally in the winter. It's called 'snow.'" I had a little fun with it. But you have to be a little sensitive. Wherever you are at in the country, it can change. Especially if you are overseas, there are a lot of things we do here that does not work there. Ask the missionary to make sure your story will translate well.

What makes an illustration effective?

You have to be concise. You can't be too long, or it overpowers the message. It is effective if it appeals to their emotions. Illustrations have to have an emotional pull. Whether it is an "Awww" about the cat who got stuck in the tree, or the swelling of gratitude and pride concerning the heroic effort by a fireman. It can be a humorous "I can relate to that" laughter that comes from, "yeah, my mom and dad did that same thing to me." It has to tug on emotions, but it is not just emotions.

It's like a doorway; something that opens into their minds so I can get them thinking. Then I'm going to slide up beside them and put these lenses on. "Now do you see that point more clearly?" David lived a long time ago, and it is hard for us to relate to a guy killing a lion and a bear to rescue a sheep. We would just say, "Enjoy the sheep. I'll go out and buy a new one." It's hard to relate to that. But I can put a lens on you to help you see this through the story of someone rescuing their puppy. I know I've got dog lovers out there. They may not be sheep lovers. But I can tell a story about somebody running into a fire to save their puppy, their kitten, or their child. If I can help them see "that's how David felt about that sheep. . . . That's how our Great Shepherd feels about His sheep." It is a more modern account of something that the audience can emotionally connect to. When they look through that frame of reference, it brings that scriptural point I am wanting to make into clearer focus to them.

What can a preacher begin doing today to improve his or her preaching?

It is my impression in working with young ministers that they really do not read the Bible. So I find that in working with inexperienced preachers or preachers who are burnt out or tired, they tend to try to find a good book or a series to preach. But if it is not in you, people know. They will know when you are rehearsing someone else's material. As simple as this sounds, I think it is important for us to consistently read the Bible—not for getting a message, but to read the Bible and figuring out "how does this speak to me?" I think if the Bible is not speaking to you—if that passage is not speaking to you—then you are not going to be able to preach it in a way that it is going to speak to someone else. Reading the Bible, absorbing it, memorizing it, and meditating on it is critical. I don't do this, but I could literally go into a counseling class right now and teach an intensive (forty-eight hours) without using a note because it is in me. It's what I do. It's how I live. It's how I think. And I think for people who are preaching the Word, It should be in them. It should be so much a part of who they are. It should be their language. It should be their thought process.

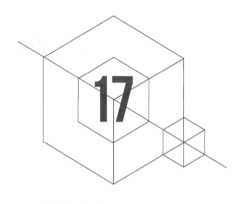

CRAFTING A
COMPELLING CONCLUSION

It was 1992, I had just graduated from high school, and the world's attention was turning to Barcelona, Spain. Athletes from around the world were boarding flights bound for the Summer Olympic Games. Derek Redmond was one of those athletes. Competing for his mother country, England, Derek looked forward to bringing home a medal.

Derek was gearing up to compete in the 400 meter race, the same race that an Achilles tendon injury had forced him to withdraw from four years earlier. This year he hoped would be different, much different. His father Jim made the trip with his son and the two agreed that no matter what happened this time, Derek was going to complete the race.

This first qualifying run would only mean Derek had to finish in the top four to advance. At the starting block, Derek cleared his mind, let the noise of the crowd fade away, and waited in anticipation for the starting gun. The shot fired and the runners were quickly in full stride. The race was going as planned. Derek was in second place and was all but assured advancement into the next round when it happened.

Derek heard a loud pop and felt excruciating pain immediately course through his right leg. He immediately went to the ground knowing his hamstring had just torn. As he knelt on the ground, the tears immediately starting flowing. He realized, yet again, he would not be allowed to compete for a medal. He surrendered to that thought only briefly and then pulled himself to his feet.

As the medical staff rushed the track, Derek motioned them away because he wanted to finish the race. As the cameras caught this picture, they also caught the desperate actions of another man in the background, Derek's father. Jim had pushed his way past security and was running to Derek. He reached Derek and put his arms around him. He told him he didn't have to finish, but his son would hear none of that. So Jim insisted, "We will finish the race together."

The crowd was standing, cheering, crying, and applauding what was happening right in front of them. The race was over, and everyone else had finished; but all eyes were on Derek and Jim. Derek crossed the finish line but didn't win a medal. However, he did win the hearts of those in attendance that day.

Yes, this true story is about the human spirit. And yes, the story highlights the resolve of those who refuse to let adversity stop them. But the story is really about finishing in spite of what happens during the race. When people tell the story of Derek, the conclusion of the race is what makes the story impacting. The finish makes the story worth telling.

Preaching is all about finishing well. The problem is, many preachers spend the least amount of time on their conclusions. But if you can learn to end well, you will be able to make up for a certain amount of deficiencies in the first part of the sermon.

A conclusion is a final summation of your thoughts. A good sermon conclusion will include the following:

1. Review – of the sermon main idea and main points.

2. Application – make appropriate application from the sermon to people's lives.

3. Direction – invite the people to make a decision based on the message you just preached and give them clear direction as to what they need to do.

A good conclusion will bring unity and clarity to the sermon and tell the audience what action should be taken in light of the sermon idea and main points. A good conclusion will be well planned and even rehearsed so that it can be done without the aid of notes. This will allow the preacher to make the application personal and better connect with the audience.

A good conclusion will call for people to make a positive decision in their lives in response to what they have heard from the Word of God that day. It is effective when we use words like, "I invite you to . . .", or "I call you to . . .", or "the Word of God invites you to . . ." and allow people to respond to the conviction they feel and the presence of God they sense around them.

A good conclusion will fit with the rest of the sermon. It is not a stand-alone piece. The audience should be able to see a profound connection to the recent parts of the sermon and see how everything ties together. Be sure to use variety in your conclusions, but make sure that your closing strategy fits the situation and the sermon you are preaching. As with the introduction, the conclusion should follow the 10-80-10 rule: Ten percent for the introduction, eighty percent for the body and ten percent for the conclusion. Thus, in a thirty minute sermon, the conclusion should be about three to four minutes long.

There are four things Dr. Ben Awbrey says are imperative for the conclusion:[37]

1. It must be composed through careful preparation.

The conclusion is the most important part of the sermon. Therefore it deserves our utmost attention in preparation. Its construction—words, phrases, and designed layout—is crucial in making that final impact on the audience.

2. It must be unmistakably personal in its aim.

The conclusion cannot be pie-in-the-sky, fairy-tale, or make-believe. The conclusion needs to touch people right where they are. It is the last opportunity for the preacher to make the biblical truth that was introduced, applicable to the listener. Don't be too general with your closing remarks. Instead be specific and concise in what you are wanting the audience to do. If you cannot explain how something is relevant to the audience, then don't share that something with them in the first place.

3. It must bring the message to a fitting end.

The conclusion should give the audience a sense of finality. Make sure there are no loose ends left untied. Most of the time you will want to avoid leaving the audience with questions in their minds. You do not want them walking away from a message confused.

4. It must affect the will and emotions of the hearers.

There is no better way to connect with the audience than by tapping into the will and emotions of the listeners. If we are aiming at persuasion—which is the goal of all sermons— then we are going to have to get them to feel something. Persuasive comments, thoughts, and questions, aimed at the will are important. However, there is no better way to grab the heart than through a story. A good clinching story can do more in a few minutes than well-crafted words trying to explain a theological idea.

It was Jesus who taught us the power of a story. The journey away from home and back by the prodigal son was emotional and gripping. The tragic experience of the lone Jewish traveler on the way from Jerusalem to Jericho, salvaged by a compassionate Samaritan, stirred the emotions of the hearers. The stories themselves taught more truth than could be disseminated by words and information alone. And when you touch the emotions, you will reap a response.

Additionally, Awbrey gives us four important elements that should be a part of every conclusion:[38]

1. A good transition to the conclusion.

Plan how you will transition to the conclusion. Craft a statement or series of statements that tie in the previous point while pointing toward a conclusion.

Learn to ease the audience into the conclusion without them knowing it. Illustrations do not need to be announced and neither does a conclusion. There will perhaps be the subtle clues of musicians stirring on the platform or even having people stand. However, you should probably start your conclusion before you have them stand. Because if you have not hooked them and do not have their buy-in, you will lose them when the distractions begin. Always remember that the person who is feeling strong conviction is looking for an easy way out.

2. Clear and forceful closing appeals justified by the development of the text.

Depending on the sermon idea, you will want to bring the biblical mandate highlighted by the subject to the forefront, strongly encouraging a response. The audience should be reminded that the Bible is not a book filled with suggestions that can be embraced or ignored. The principles outlined in Scripture are keys to either eternal life or eternal separation from God. If there is something to be obeyed, then the preacher should strongly encourage obedience and rebuke disobedience.

3. Appeal to unbelievers for repentance and conversion.

Every sermon should reach for the unbeliever. The opportunity for repentance should be made available whether you feel someone needs to repent or not. The possibility of conversion should be encouraged every time you preach. Hopefully God has led people to the service who do not know the Lord and they need to put their faith in Him. Each sermon should be created with space allowed for preaching to sinners.

4. Clinching element of persuasion.

How do you plan to drive home that purpose you set out to accomplish from the very beginning? How will you grip them, challenge them, and pull them from their discouragement, their problems, their despair, and their doubt? This will take prayer, preparation, and creativity. This will take work to craft something that is not just thrown together. Thankfully the Lord comes through at times with thoughts and ideas you were not even considering during preparation. And He allows you to persuade the audience because of the leading of the Spirit. However, we all know this does not happen every single time because the Lord does not want us to become negligent in our preparation.

INTERVIEW

WITH

WAYNE HUNTLEY

Below are comments taken from an interview with Wayne Huntley, pastor of The Temple of Pentecost (Raleigh, North Carolina), on the topic of crafting compelling conclusions:

What are the important things that come to mind when you think about closing out a message?

The key to being successful is your sensitivity to the Holy Ghost, the Spirit. You must be sensitive to the pulse of the sinner, when you sense conviction on them. One thing that makes many preachers and evangelists ineffective is that they are more impressed with how they are delivering the sermon than they are with what is happening in the sinner. Sometimes we preach past conviction. If you preach past conviction, you are in deep trouble. When conviction is obvious, you close that message because your goal is not to preach a masterpiece. Your job is to get that sinner to make a decision. You have to move with sensitivity to the Spirit and sensitivity to your audience.

The conclusion should come when you have captured the hearts of both saints and sinners. For an effective altar appeal, you need conviction on the sinner and cooperation from the saints. What we stand behind is called a "Pul-pit." The preacher is pulling people from the pit. I have trained my church that when I begin to pull people from the pit, you push from the pew. By pushing I mean, they are pushing in the Spirit, in intercession, in burden, and in faith. So if I am pulling and the church is pushing, we have a greater opportunity to be successful. If the pulpit does not have pull, then the pit will be full.

If you are preaching with illustrations, your strongest one should be saved until last. And if that one doesn't work, then "Houston, we have a problem." You are building toward the conclusion. You are step by step moving them. You are gradually pushing them and nudging them so that when you make that final appeal they are ready to come.

Must every sermon demand an altar call?

No. There are a variety of sermons. Sometimes we are sowing seed or building faith for the future. You may not really be making a conclusive appeal for people to make a decision today.

I don't feel the need for the traditional altar call in today's society. I move mostly in, "Bring a friend to the front. Let's all come to the front. We all need God." I don't think there is any virtue in people being humiliated by walking down the aisle alone and being singled out. I don't see any virtue in that at all. "While Peter yet spake these words, the Holy Ghost fell." There was no altar call.

INTERVIEW

WITH

TOM FOSTER

Below are comments taken from an interview with Tom Foster, pastor of Dallas First Church (Dallas, Texas), on the topic of crafting compelling conclusions:

What are some important things that come to mind in closing out a message?

You know how Jesus would tell a story, even God in the Old Testament? He always started with the conclusion. He talked to Moses and Joshua as if they were already where He wanted them to be and then worked backwards. So with a message I am always looking for, "Where are we going?" "What do I want to see happen?" And then work backwards. Because if I don't know where I am going how do I know where to start? I keep the conclusion in mind.

When I started preaching, I watched preachers. I watched them preach to the point where it should be ending, but then they would preach right through it. They preached the anointing off and the sermon died.

Sometimes we think, *I have another page of notes here.* But you don't have to finish your message because they are ready to respond now. I learned that on the evangelistic field: you don't have to finish a message. Now pastoring for thirty years that is probably one of the hardest parts of preaching because you just know they need that next point. "Now don't stop me now, you need to hear this message." But I have learned that the next Sunday rolls around really quickly so I can take that point I didn't preach last Sunday and make another message out of it.

What makes an effective conclusion?

To sum it all up would be: an action. But to get there, sometimes it is pointed, clear, and straightforward. At other times you let them figure it out and let them think about it.

You want that message with its conclusion to be relevant to their life, and what they can do. So if it is to give time, to give of their ability, to give money, to gain victory, to commit, or come to this altar and take up a new life. So in that conclusion, there is going to be a shifting and a restlessness in the audience. They are going to feel as if they have to do something—I can't sit here much longer. And if you miss it, then you have to build it all over again.

A lot of times we don't prepare for our endings. I like to offer them something. Even on our midweek teaching nights, I'm going to prepare them for an altar service. I don't want them to treat the altar area like it is a foreign country. I want them to be familiar with it.

Should every sermon demand an altar call?

I think it should demand an action. I don't want to waste somebody's time. The reason I am preaching is to move you. I am preaching to inspire you. I am preaching to educate you. I am preaching to help you. But mainly I am preaching for your potential. A lot of time in our preaching, we are preaching to the problem.

When I was an evangelist, the problem was I preached to their problems. When I started pastoring, I preached to problems. After I had been here several years, I realized I needed to shift gears. After about seven years it dawned on me, "If I just think problems and preach to problems, I'm always going to have problems. But if I can get everyone to look at their potential—what are they becoming, where are they going, what is happening with them—then we can have victory. So each message has a potential. We cannot waste it at the ending.

I feel like a lot of times we lose that at an altar call by not giving one. If you have fifty, five hundred, or a thousand, someone is there needing what you are preaching about. They have potential, no matter how down they are, no matter how bad they've been, no matter how life has been cruel to them, abused them, or mistreated them. Everybody has potential. Oscar Wilde said, "Every saint has a past, every sinner has a future."

Remind them of their potential. They can be a better dad, mother, son, daughter, employer, employee, student, teacher, citizen, or soldier for God. They can be better.

Why do you think some churches are abandoning that altar call?

This is a movement and it is going in a direction I do not like. Nowadays the average sinner is no different from the average church member—taking into account all the churches in America. There is not that much difference, so they don't have to have an altar call.

I was in conversation with a pastor of a megachurch in Dallas. They run about twenty thousand weekly, and he doesn't give altar calls. He said, "Tom, I don't care what the people do during the week, as long as they are there on Sunday in their place. That is what I am after."

So instead of an altar call, that is where they take their offering, sell product in their bookstore, etc. It is more of a performance. So people come like you would go to the movies. When you go to the movies, you go in, sit down, and watch the show. You become whatever the actor is doing and you win the victory. But when the lights come up, you walk right back out and you are fighting that same battle—that movie didn't help you at all.

I don't want church to become just another show, just another performance, just another going through the motions. And I'm afraid that's what we are becoming. That's why Jesus, every time He talked about the second coming, half the church was lost. That is why I am wanting to move the people to action, to make a difference. We are different. If we are children of God then we seek first His kingdom and His righteousness.

How do you stay motivated to preach on a regular basis even when you are tired, stressed, or just plain lacking the "want to"?

Sometimes you don't have a choice. Sometimes I am motivated by the fact that they will be gathering together at noon on Sunday and I better have something from the Word to share. I also think preachers ought to have a plan in place where there is another voice that they can bring to their pulpit, because we need rest. I think one of the saddest things is the lack of "self-care" among the ministry; that they have this sense of "it's ok to recuperate. It's ok that I am not on 24/7." I think that is very sad that they feel the whole world is going to fall apart if they don't show up.

If you are not in a good place in your own walk with God that will leak out in the pulpit. It's not so much about being motivated to get up and preach another sermon, but how am I in the presence of God all week long leading up to that sermon I am going to be preaching? Because now I need Him more than I have ever needed Him. As simple as this is, I think people who love God, who are preaching His Word, and are pastoring the flocks, they are not spending time with God. They are so busy doing His work that they don't have time to spend with Him. And He enables us by His grace. He is the wisdom when we lack wisdom. He is strength when we are weak. He is help when we have no other resource. He is the Source. And I think forgetting that puts us in a very vulnerable position. But I think for people who know that, come Monday I better be centering myself, I better sit down and not start working on next Sunday's message but I'm just in the presence of the Lord for the grace that He alone can give and He supplies the strength. He supplies the energy. He supplies the creativity. And He gives the great ideas.

THE APPLICATION
AND CALL TO ACTION

After recognizing a continual struggle with idolatry and the pull of their past lives, Joshua called all the Israelites together at Shechem. This was significant because this was the very place God had initiated His covenant with Abraham. (See Genesis 12:6-7.) The church should be a place that regularly reminds us of the covenant we have entered into with the Lord. That covenant and our commitment to that covenant should be motivating factors in the decisions we make to keep living for Jesus Christ.

Joshua preached a convicting message of commitment and consecration that day at Shechem. He reminded them of their father Abraham and how God had brought him and his family out of idolatry and into the land of Canaan. (See Joshua 24:2-3.) Joshua spoke to them of how God had preserved Isaac, Jacob, and their fathers in Egypt. (See Joshua 24:4.) The people stood still, listening to every word, as he continued to talk about Moses, Aaron, their ancestors' deliverance from Egypt and their wilderness wanderings. (See Joshua 24:5-7.)

Joshua continued to preach about God's power, deliverance, and the victory He had given them over the Amorites and the Moabites. (See Joshua 24:8-10.) He reminded them of how God had brought them safely over Jordan and had given Jericho into their hands. (See Joshua 24:11-12.)

And in verse thirteen, I can hear Joshua calling for the musicians to come.

The stage had been set. Joshua had highlighted God's greatness and allowed them to be reminded of His power, providence, and provision. But he also turned the mood as He caused them to understand they had not achieved success by their own might. The victory had not come because they were strong or even holy. They were in a place of favor because God had extended mercy and had continued to honor His covenant even if they hadn't.

As the keyboardist began to play and the singers got into place, Joshua launched into his appeal:

"Now therefore fear the LORD and serve him in sincerity and in faithfulness. Put away the gods that your fathers served beyond the River and in Egypt, and serve the LORD. And if it is evil in your eyes to serve the LORD, choose this day whom you will serve, whether the gods your fathers served in the region beyond the River, or the gods of the Amorites in whose land you dwell. But as for me and my house, we will serve the LORD" (Joshua 24:14-15, ESV).

The Lord anointed Joshua that day and the response of the people proved God had touched their hearts. The message he had delivered out of obedience to the Lord was clear and convicting. By the time Joshua had given the challenge, the people were ready to respond with a God-honoring decision.

The point of decision is accomplished by applying at minimum, three elements:

1. The application
2. The call to action
3. The call to prayer

Joshua made continual application throughout his message by tying the Israelites in his audience to the Israelite actions of the past. Example after example showed the people how the decision they were needing to make was tied to the decisions of Abraham, Isaac, Jacob, Moses, and their fathers who had been led out of slavery in Egypt. Joshua linked them to the covenant, reminding them of their own commitment and consecration. Then he could challenge them to act.

The scene cannot get any more dramatic than this: an aging leader wearing his heart on his sleeve and pleading with a people who were on the verge of throwing their covenant away. He had appealed to the memories of the past and now called them to take action in the present.

Extending his staff, Joshua lowered one end until it settled into the dusty earth near his feet. Then slowly, but methodically, the old man began shuffling to his left, leaving the end of his staff to drag the dirt in front of him. Establishing a line of boundary, Joshua called to the people. "You have a choice today. Either stay on that side and serve the idols of this world or rid yourselves of everything that is not of God, and serve the LORD. But as for me and my house, we are going to serve the LORD."

His call to action was clear. To respond to what God was asking, there would need to be decisive action taken. A choice would need to be made. This choice would involve both forsaking and embracing. Forsaking the things of the world and embracing the purpose of God for their lives. The people responded by declaring their allegiance to the Lord and removing the idols from the camp. (See Joshua 24:16-24.)

Though there is not an explicit call to prayer found in this passage, there is a call to renewal of the covenant. (See Joshua 24:25-27.) Not every sermon will end with an altar call, but most of the time there should be an opportunity for prayerful consideration at the end of a message. People need some time to process what has been said and what they are going to do once they leave that atmosphere. At times, the solemnness of the commitment and the moment need to be reflected upon.

In fact, Joshua told the people, "I am putting this stone here beneath this tree as a testimony of your commitment today. This will also be a witness against you if you should ever go back on your word to God." (See Joshua 24:27.) We must realize the seriousness of the covenant and our commitment to it. Our word to God should mean something.

The Three Elements

The audience must see how the message applies to their lives. What should they do from this point forward? How should they respond to what they have heard? How does this affect them after they leave the sanctuary?

1. The Application

First of all, we must recognize that the Scriptures we have today had all been written by the end of the first century. The authors of these books had in mind the hearers of that day when they wrote each word. We can apply the truths we find to our lives, but we must remember it was not written specifically to us. This is one reason why it is critical we do not simply search Scripture for words and phrases that fit what we are looking to illustrate and launch into a sermon tirade without a concern for context.

There is only one interpretation for the verses you are reading. Thankfully many applications can be drawn from each. However, if we do not first concern ourselves with interpretation, we may find ourselves off the deep end when it comes to application.

One Scripture I hear quoted frequently is Matthew 18:20: "For where two or three are gathered together in my name, there am I in the midst of them."

Context: This verse is found at the end of a section on how to deal with a believer who has offended another believer. The offended believer is admonished to privately confront the one who has sinned against them in order to make amends. The passage then goes on to detail what should happen if the offender either repents or chooses to ignore the situation. One such recommendation is for the offended person to bring two or three witnesses with him should the offender not respond in the private confrontation.

208

This section wraps up with the statement, "For where two or three gather together as my followers, I am there among them" (NLT). In other words, if we follow the correct scriptural response in handling offenses, God will be with us, in our midst, to assist us in the process.

Common application: Truthfully, I have never heard this verse in its proper context. Instead, we use it to encourage ourselves when we come to church and realize half of the congregation is either home sick or out of town. "Well, though there may not be many of us here today, we can be sure of one thing, God is here. Because the Bible tells us, 'If two or three are gathered together in His name, Jesus is there!'"

Result: This application does not necessarily disagree with the entirety of Scripture. However, it does have the possibility of leading us to some negative results. Number one, it can lead us to forgetting the truth being discussed in this passage of Matthew. In fact, churches have so overly quoted verse 20—out of context—that they hardly see a reason to discuss verses 15-19. Secondly, this application can also lead someone to doubt if God will meet with them at moments when they are alone. When in fact, Scripture is replete with examples of God coming alongside someone who was by themselves.

You do not need two or three to gather with you in order to find God right there beside you. But it might be a good idea for us to highlight the importance of asking Jesus to gather with us as we handle potential conflicts and disputes with our brothers and sisters. Maybe we would avoid some hurt feelings and severed relationships that often occur when we think we can handle it all on our own.

"Application is part of the preacher's responsibility."[39]

As a twenty-first century preacher, you are charged to make the truth applicable to those living in the modern world. You must wrestle with principles and how they are to be embraced by those in your audience. Preaching is more than just telling them what the Bible says. It also involves helping them understand how the teachings of the Bible fit into their everyday lives.

"Application is needed by the congregation."[40]

Just as Joshua did for the Israelites (Joshua 24), the preacher needs to show the audience how their condition is connected to the overall plan of God. They need to understand how the words of Paul relate to their situation. Sometimes it is obvious, but the responsibility still rests with us to make it as clear as possible.

"The application of Truth is the purpose of Scripture."[41]

"For whatsoever things were written aforetime were written for our learning, that we through patience and comfort of the Scriptures might have hope" (Romans 15:4). We have hope when we see that the declarations of the Bible were not only given to the early church, but we also can embrace them for ourselves.

In order to determine a correct application of Scripture, a few things need to be considered. Ask yourself, "What does this passage teach me about God? The church? The world? About myself and my desires and motives?" You may also look closely to determine if there is a particular action we should be taking or decision we should be making. Perhaps the passage is calling us to repentance or confession of some sin in our lives. Answers to these questions will help you in formulating a biblical application for yourself and your audience.

Relate the truth you have gleaned to the basic human needs and problems experienced by individuals today. When you can take God's Word and apply it to where individuals are hurting and struggling, the final step in the sermon (call to action) becomes much easier.

Use illustrations that will help show how the truth you are sharing can be applied in day-to-day living. Application implies action. If you can show them how what you are preaching can be applied tomorrow when they get up for work, the Word of God will come alive to them.

Awbrey lists several different areas of applicable content when applying truth from Scripture and each sermon point. Is there sin to confess? A promise to claim? An attitude to change? A command to obey? An example to follow? A prayer to pray? An error to avoid? A truth to believe? Or something to praise God for?

Once we have determined these, it's time for Joshua to call the musicians and make his call to action.

2. The Call to Action

As we found in Joshua 24, the elder leader had preached a message filled with application. He had challenged the mindset of Israel and shown them the error of their ways. Once he felt they were ready, he dared them to take the right action. "Choose you this day who you will serve!"

A sermon without a call to action will leave the audience in limbo, not really understanding the reason they just sat through the last forty-five-minute sermon. The call to action becomes the "point" you were striving for when you began putting this message together. Your goal was to persuade the audience to "do something."

Did you want them to repent and turn from sin? Were you wanting them to decide to surrender to God, to offer worship, or to express faith in a particular way?

When Peter began preaching on the day of Pentecost, his purpose was to bring his audience to a place of decision. After hearing him, they were going to decide whether or not they would embrace Jesus as Messiah. The incredible thing about Peter's message was that it was relatively unplanned and extemporaneous. However, a clear path to a crucial decision and call to action was evident. The Holy Spirit was in control and was going to show all of us what a truly, Spirit-anointed message would look like for the church. Such a message will have Jesus as the focus. And when man's words come to an end, the Spirit will prick hearts.

Peter's goal—actually the Spirit's goal—was accomplished. Because when he finished and gave his final thoughts, the audience was ready to respond.

"Men and brethren, what shall we do?" (Acts 2:37).

Peter's call to action: "Repent and be baptized, every one of you, in the name of Jesus Christ, for the remission of sins, and ye shall receive the gift of the Holy Ghost . . . Save yourselves from this untoward generation" (Acts 2:38, 40).

When Peter was done, the audience knew what it was going to take to embrace Jesus as Messiah. And over three thousand did just that.

3. The Call to Prayer

The very place Joshua called the people to renew their covenant, was the very place Abraham had first received the covenant, built an altar, and called on the name of the Lord. This coming Sunday morning, when you give a call to prayer—or an altar call—the people may not be standing at Shechem. But as they bow to their knees, lift their hands, and call on the name of the Lord, they are experiencing the benefits of that same covenant.

Not every sermon will demand an altar call—in the traditional sense—but every sermon should lead to prayer. Whether you are wanting the people to decide to repent or rejoice, surrender or express faith, you will want them to call on the name of the Lord.

What is the most important part of the sermon?

For me, it's the conclusion. I feel like I want to set it up well and I want to deliver the heart of it well. But if at the end there is not something they connect with and respond to . . . When we have an encounter with truth, there should be a "Lord, is it me?" Kind of like with the disciples when Jesus said, "One of you will betray me." And they went down the line, "Is it me? Is it me?" I think that should be the ending. When truth is spoken then the congregation has that moment when they say, "Are you talking to me? Is this me?" And I am hoping to deliver the message in a way that each person in that congregation asks that question: "Is it me? Is this for me? What part of this was for me?" And then they respond.

IV

SERMON DELIVERY

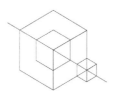

PREACHING
WITHOUT NOTES

The goal of preaching is to boldly declare and effectively communicate the gospel of Jesus Christ—working hand in hand with the Holy Ghost—so those who hear the Word may be saved. If preaching is this important, then it doesn't really matter whether you choose to use notes or not use notes. What matters most is that whatever you do is effective.

The most popular methods of sermon preparation being taught in both Bible schools and seminaries are outlining, manuscripting, or a combination of the two. However, maybe we are overlooking a method that could be even more effective. Though I personally feel we have to choose the method we feel most comfortable with, find out for yourself whether you are preaching a certain way because that is all you have known or because it truly is the best way for you to communicate the gospel.

Many would argue that notes are required so that you know exactly what you want to say whereas without notes you may forget some details. However, proponents of preaching without notes would argue that notes keep you from being conversational and distract you from truly sensing where your audience is and how the Holy Spirit is moving during the message delivery.

John Albiston discusses his take on preaching without notes:

"The truth is that you already know what you're talking about, you've already invested hours of prayer and study, and it's just a matter of delivery. That being said, there are a number of techniques you can use to ease your way into this."[42]

Two of his suggestions are:

1. Start with a narrative passage.

Starting with a biblical narrative as the foundation for our sermon will allow us to tap into our natural ability to relate stories. We have been created by God to learn much easier through the use of stories. Every society has a story, a narrative they tell to succeeding generations.

2. Hide your notes in plain sight.

Knowing the story will help you stay on track and ultimately communicate the message of the sermon. "You need to meditate and emotionally immerse yourself in the text in such a way that the story comes to life in full color and sound. If you try merely reciting the facts of the story like a man trying to remember a grocery list, you'll end up forgetting things and put your people to sleep while you're doing so."[43]

Secondly, employ the use of technology. Since not every message will lend itself to preaching solely through a narrative, you may need some notes. Having a PowerPoint slide for each point or statement of emphasis will allow you to refer to your "notes" without being tied to an iPad or notepad. "This will work best if you have the remote in your own pocket. All you have to do is discreetly push a button, and your next point will appear for all to see. You then talk about that point and when you're done, push the button for your next point. You will have the best of both worlds. You'll be able to engage your congregation fully, and you'll never miss anything important."[44]

In order to preach successfully without notes, the preacher will need to do a certain amount of memorization. It is not recommended that you memorize everything word for word, because you could still come across the same way a manuscript sermon would—rehearsed and wooden. However, whether it be the narrative itself, your outline, or a handful of main points, the preacher will need to spend time getting to know the material well enough to deliver it smoothly.

"Remember, if you don't remember it, they aren't going to remember it."[45]

William Carl also suggests some ideas to aid the preacher in memorizing key points of the sermon:

"If you want to remember two to three paragraphs, take one word out of each paragraph that summarizes that paragraph. Put that word on the right side of the page, and circle it. On the left side of the page, put a picture that will represent (or trigger) the paragraph."[46]

Preaching without notes is not a shortcut to avoid study and preparation. In fact, those who preach without notes may have to spend a little more time internalizing the message than those who will rely on an outline or manuscript. Again, neither method is better than the other, though proponents of both sides might argue there is. The crucial question you must answer is, "How can I best communicate what God has given me?"

INTERVIEW

WITH

JOEL URSHAN

Below are comments taken from an interview with Joel Urshan, pastor of First Apostolic Church (Cincinnati, Ohio), on the topic of preaching without notes:

Have you always preached without notes?

I have not. The notes I used to use were very unorthodox. I basically had one sheet of paper. Very rarely did it go over onto a second page. I had an introduction and some points for the body of the message that would bring me to the conclusion. I still didn't use it much while I was preaching because I did not like to rely on them. I didn't start preaching without notes until about five or six years ago. When I teach, I will have a list of Scriptures that I will use. I did not intentionally start preaching without notes, but it happened over time.

I vividly remember one particular service. I was getting ready to preach; and during the worship service, the message quickly took form in my mind. It was like the Lord did it. He placed it in my mind, in mental form, as though it were notes. It has happened like that ever since. It was never something I deliberately did. It just happened that way.

How do you map out the sermon in your mind?

It is common for me to go to the platform without having everything in place in my mind. But I have developed a confidence that all the pieces will come together. And it happens every time now. It doesn't excuse prayer, scriptures, and study. It still requires all of that. And the more you do those things, the better prepared you are to preach. If you don't, you are really taking a risk. There is the possibility of getting up there and falling flat on your face because it really is a spiritual thing.

J. T. Pugh once said, "If you want to find me before I preach, I will be somewhere speaking in tongues." As a young man, that really resonated with me. He was describing that this is where his confidence came from and where God would put things together for him.

Do you see any cons in preaching without notes?

Without notes, sometimes a preacher can give too much explanation, and can elaborate too much, going beyond the bounds of what is necessary. You want to make sure you do not disseminate everything you know about a particular story, example, or illustration. Just use what fits for that message and let the other stuff go, even if it is good stuff. Notes will help you do that. Without notes you have to be very purposeful to do that.

Do you see a difference between memorizing and putting to memory?

There are passages of Scripture that I will purposely put to memory. There are some things I quote routinely in my sermons. I love quoting John 1, Hebrews 11, Psalm 1, and Luke 12. I enjoy quoting excerpts from Patrick Henry's speech, "Give me liberty, or give me death." There are certain things like that I think are good to infuse in the message. It doesn't need to dominate the whole message, but it is effective to infuse it a quarter of the way or half-way through, and have some recitation. When you string several verses together as something coming from your soul, it really creates awareness that Scripture is full of powerful truth that can change our lives.

INTERVIEW

JASON SCISCOE

Below are comments taken from an interview with Jason Sciscoe, pastor of The Church Triumphant (Pasadena, Texas), on the topic of preaching without notes:

Have you always preached without notes? Has that always been your style?

No. I experimented and went through a journey. When preachers first start preaching, they preach basically how they've watched other people preach. A preacher will see his favorite preachers, people that influenced him, and then watch what they do.

Personally, I tried to do the Anthony Mangun style—word for word—because I liked how he didn't waste any words. That was so important to me and so I really tried to do that. My problem was, I would get into the middle of the message and the Holy Ghost would start moving. A lot of things that I wasn't expecting to say, but felt directed to say, would come to mind and so I would say them. Then I could never find my way back to my place in my notes. And so, I would end up having to wing the last several minutes, because nothing fit after I had deviated from the page.

I found myself thinking, "Well, maybe what I could do is write a word-for-word introduction to at least get me started. Then once that gets me to my main point, I'll write two or three main points down on a page, followed by my ending. That worked for a while. But I still kept feeling like, "I don't have freedom. I don't have liberty. I'm not really ministering. I'm not really connecting with people. I'm still too mechanical. My thoughts are not original enough." So I literally sat down after two or three years of preaching and said, "I have to figure out a philosophy of preaching and what my philosophy was going to be going forward. And I need to commit to that if I'm going to do this, or else I'm going to be frustrated.

I sat down and started researching the Gospels. I started researching every sermon in the New Testament. And I noticed that they didn't seem to be that planned. Peter standing up with the eleven said, "Ye men and brethren, these men are not drunk as ye suppose." This was not a planned sermon. He heard people ask questions and he answered their questions. And while he was answering their questions, the Holy Ghost fell on them. He started quoting Scripture, put it together, and he had three thousand people converted from that one message on the Day of Pentecost.

I don't think there were any notes there. I don't think that was planned. I think that was just the Holy Ghost leading. I started looking at other Scriptures in the Bible where the apostles preached, Paul preached, or Jesus preached, and I found a few other places where it appeared to be very planned out. For instance, Stephen's message was planned. He had it together. He knew his material extremely well. My conclusion was that the issue was not notes or no notes. The issue was, "What works best to accomplish the goal? What is going to help me to flow the best?" And so the conclusion I came to was: if I don't know the material well enough to just stand up and talk about it, then I probably don't need to be talking about it.

I realize there are a lot of people who know their material very well, and their notes just facilitate that knowledge. However, I found that notes distracted me. For me, I'm not supposed to preach with notes. This is my discipline, and I have to do this by faith. I finally became locked into a certain style at that point, and I started getting better at it.

So how do you prepare? Is there a way you map it out? Do you have a template you normally follow?

Absolutely. One hundred percent. You can hide behind, "I don't preach with notes because I'm spiritual." Or you can say, "I don't preach with notes because I don't think it's necessary." And sometimes, you're just lazy. You're going to just extemporaneously talk off the top of your head, and it was nice; but come on—if you would've really applied yourself, it could've been a stellar sermon. Instead, it was okay. That's not what this is about.

This is a discipline I learned after doing all the preparation; spending hours and hours and hours on one sermon. I went through a period where I did all the due diligence, I wrote the introduction. I wrote point A and point B. I wrote the subpoints underneath point A, B, and C. I wrote conclusions. I learned the discipline of preparing the message. What happened was after I did that, I took those homiletical principles and said, "Now I want to cultivate this in the way God is using me and where I feel most comfortable."

I am an expository preacher. My philosophy is, "preach the Word." I am not starting with a story I heard and then looking for a Scripture. My first goal was to know the Bible inside and out. So I have a working knowledge of every chapter in the Bible. I don't necessarily know every verse, but I have a working knowledge of every chapter in the Bible. To do this, I got the Bible on CD—now it's on my iPad and my iPhone—and I listen to the text over and over and over until I have volumes of information of the Word of God in my spirit.

What the Lord told me early on was, "I can't talk to you about things you don't know. I can't tell you what Psalm 46 means if you don't know what it says." So that became my first goal: to really master the Scriptures. So until I feel I have a grasp on what that Scripture is talking about, I'm not going to preach on that Scripture.

The next thing that I do is focus on the audience I'm going to be addressing. "What do they need, God? What are You wanting to accomplish in this service?" I'm praying, "God I need you to speak to me." Then He speaks a verse to me. He speaks a story to me. He brings something to my mind. And oh wow! Now that I have the specific example He wants me to focus on, I research that topic upside down, inside out, and I put that one thing in my spirit.

When I develop my outline, I find that I often look at a story. And because principles are communicated through people, I would always use a person. Instead of using an idea, I would use a person to illustrate the idea. For example, take a simple message I preached from I Samuel 17, on the narrative of David leaving home to visit his brothers while they were in battle. The passage tells us David left the sheep with the keeper (verse 20), he left the carriage with the keeper (verse 22), and then after seeing the giant, he didn't leave the giant to anybody else. He said, "No, I'm going to take care of this giant. Somebody else can take care of the sheep. Somebody else can take care of the carriage. But I am the only one that can take care of the giant." I preached: "Keeper of the Giant."

I talk about the difference between a train track preacher and a sailboat preacher. A train track preacher is someone that cannot deviate from their text at all. The only thing you do on a train track is slow down or speed up. A train track preacher is on a track and he knows where he's going. All he does is slow down or speed up based on response.

I'm a sailboat preacher. I know where I'm going, but I'm going to factor in wind and waves. I might go a little bit this way, a little bit that way. I'm going to get there, but there might be a reason God would redirect me toward saying this or that. I'm discerning the hearts and the minds of the people. That's why I get down off the platform. I get down to where the people are, because I'm reading them. My idea is not to impress you with how good of a preacher I am. My idea is I'm supposed to be communicating the Word of God to you. I'm supposed to be connecting with you. That's my primary goal.

What do you see as the pros of preaching without notes? And what do you see as the cons of preaching without notes?

Cons: You don't have as much specific clarity about how you are going to end a message or maybe how you are

225

going to begin a message when you preach without notes. I pray, "God help me know how to open this and how to close this." I know where I am going and what I want to get accomplished. I know what I am going to be speaking. However, when someone preaches with notes, I find they can be very specific and can have a little more artistry. It is much easier to use alliterations and direct quotes. If you have notes, you know what your ending is; and you know what your beginning is. If you don't have notes, you have to work harder at intros and conclusions.

Pros: It puts you in that place in the Spirit where you trust the Holy Ghost and you have total confidence. I have a security every time I preach now because I know I am in the Word. I know that everything I do is the Word of God. Or else I don't preach. So I don't feel like it is my opinion, or it's me trying to persuade you with a good argument. That is the only thing—the Word of God is the Source.

There were so many times when I was first pastoring that people would say, "That was a phenomenal message." And I'm smiling, thinking "You have no idea how little I started with." I started with a title, a scripture, and a main thought of what I felt like God wanted me to say. And while I was going, the words came. While I was preaching, the revelation came. While I was going, the illustrations would come. Because I had done the prayer and research in the past, I could pull from that. God would direct me to "Say this now; do this now." The reason I have people pray during my message is its processing time. I'll stop and say, "Let's stop and lift our hands right now, and let's thank the Lord for His Word." And when they are doing that, I'm resetting. Okay, let's not get on a rabbit trail. Let's not get off. What's our text? What's our story? What are we working on? Where are the people? I'm assessing. I'm processing and then God is saying: "Do this." I'm hearing the voice of God just stream through me and I'm just repeating what He's saying.

That is a discipline that comes by doing it continually. It started back in those early days when I would preach with notes. The Holy Ghost would start moving, and I would just step out and trust Him. But my endings would be horrible because I was so abrupt. I wouldn't know where to end because I had no more notes on what I had just said.

What would your advice be to a preacher that says, "I want to preach without notes?"

My advice would be, don't just do it because I do it or because somebody else does it. First of all, you need to do it because it is really the style God has given you. Secondly, if you do really want to preach this way, then it requires you to put in the hours of study and knowing the Word of God, zeroing in on what particular text God is wanting you to preach from. Once you get your text, research that specific text and keep it simple. Instead of trying to be profound, the idea is to be a communicator. Good communicators make complicated things simple. You are trying to take this text and break it down in order to help people know three things: What does the text say? What does the text mean? What does it mean to the audience?

The second thing you do is you engage all of your five senses in the text. Ask yourself, "What's going on? Why is it going on? What do you see? What do you hear? What do you feel? Is there something to taste? Is there something to touch?" Look around. Check the time frames. I want to pop my head right into the text. If it's Daniel, I want to see the lions. I want to know how deep the pit is. I want to know everything. So when I'm preaching it, I'm knowledgeable of the entire text.

When I come into that Scripture, I can be comfortable preaching without notes because I know what God is trying to say, I know the text, and I know how I'm going to apply it.

I suggest people start with a simple outline or a simple idea. You can write down ideas. Write down thoughts. Write down revelations. It doesn't mean you don't ever write anything down (to preach without notes). Don't tie yourself down by saying, "Since I don't use notes, I can never use notes" to be a purist. But to go down this road, this is what you have to do: You have to memorize Scripture, you have to learn the text, and you have to be comfortable speaking in this form of extemporaneous and expository speaking.

What are three things a preacher can begin doing today to improve their preaching?

1. Acquire a passion for the Word. Fall in love with the Word, not just to preach it but to assimilate it into your life; to let the Word be made flesh and dwell in you. Get a passion to read it and to believe its promises, to obey its instructions, to heed its warnings, to follow its examples, to truly let it become the greatest passion of your life.

2. Acquire a passion to hear His voice. Learn to love silence. At some point, you have to turn everything off and even in your prayer life just be still and learn to hear that still, small voice of God. My simple philosophy in life is what Jesus said, "My sheep hear my voice and follow me." He wants us to hear His voice. It shouldn't be some mystical, weird, rare occurrence. He wants to talk to us. But we have to have a passion for it. We have to want to hear it.

3. As confirmations of your call come, write them down and date them. When someone speaks something to you or if God gives you a Scripture about your calling in life, write it down. I have about thirty pages of things like this written down. Rarely do I get up to speak that I haven't read through those thoughts. And I will say, "God, You said this. And I am saying, 'Amen.' This was not my idea. I didn't ask to do this. I wanted to be a professor of English in an Ivy League college. This was Your idea. And so I am standing now, not just on the message I am going to speak; but I am standing on what You said. I'm going to this pulpit in confidence; not in my own preparation, not in my own abilities. I am trusting in three things: Your call, Your anointing, and Your promises." That's just how I step to the pulpit.

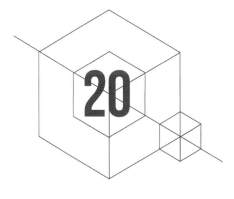

PREACHING FROM A MANUSCRIPT

No one preaches on day one the exact same way they will be preaching when they deliver their final sermon fifty years in the future. Still, everyone has to start somewhere. Only you can define what your preferred style is and how you best communicate the truth God has given you to share. And to determine this will take time, practice, and making a few mistakes along the way.

I have been impacted by messages preachers have preached with notes and without notes. The common factor between all of them was they knew how to use Scripture, passion, and all the other elements of a sermon to move their audience.

Just like anything else, your preaching style will develop over time through trial and error. My personal opinion is that anyone new to preaching will want to begin preparing sermons at least by scripting both the introduction and conclusion and then outlining the major points or thoughts they wish to focus on. This does not mean you will preach directly from the manuscript, reading it word for word—though some of you will—but the process of creating the manuscript will prove to be of tremendous value. It is crucial for beginners to learn how to develop a thought and lay it out in a logical, understandable flow. Whether your style ends up being outline, no notes, or manuscript, your style won't matter if you do not know how to put together a message your audience can understand and follow.

Preparing a manuscript—actually writing out everything you would say word for word—will cause the preacher to spend a significant amount of time determining exactly how he would like to present every point, every idea, every illustration, and every word. This "results in a more well-crafted and thoughtful presentation of God's word than might otherwise be offered."[47]

The one argument I hear over and over against using a manuscript is a preacher who uses limited or no notes will be able to have much better eye contact with the congregation, and thus, the congregation will be more engaged. I don't necessarily buy that argument. In fact, I have seen manuscript preachers actually be more engaging at times than those who do not use a manuscript.

Manuscript preachers will, over time, learn how to present themselves and their message without being so tied to their text, thus avoiding the danger of forgetting they even have an audience out there. Skilled manuscript preachers will learn to read without the audience being distracted by their reading. There is a cadence and rhythm that is learned. If the sermon is interesting, the audience will stay tuned no matter the style.

"When preachers provide well-prepared and articulated sermons, there is a greater potential for parishioners to receive a worthwhile body of persuasion and instruction."[48] One reason for this is due to the variety of word usage that can be applied because they have thought out everything ahead of time. If you are like me, I have a limited vocabulary, especially when I am extemporaneously talking. I often revert to using the same words, the same phrases, and the same adjectives when discussing and talking about things with others.

A preacher who delivers a message without notes will most likely end up utilizing "the same terminology over and over simply because the on-the-spot vocabulary of most of us in American society today is not as broad as we might wish."[49] Many of us have problems giving our undivided attention to someone speaking for an extended period of time who does not use language that is well-crafted and descriptive. In fact, the potential for the audience to retain information is a lot higher when they are presented information in a creative and articulate way.

Another reason a preacher may wish to use a manuscript is to ensure they do not say something off-the-cuff they would end up kicking themselves for afterwards. Of course, this doesn't make it foolproof. I have personally gotten tongue-tied with a manuscript before and said some pretty embarrassing things. But I guess my chances are dramatically diminished by planning out my words in advance.

In Pentecost, we hunger for those moments when God speaks through us, directing us to say things we had not prepared beforehand. Those moments are powerful and can produce a breakthrough in the middle of a message. However, we have had those moments when we felt like what we were saying was not getting through. In an effort to make something happen, we stepped away from our notes and began speaking "from the heart." How many times has your heart betrayed you and led you to say something you wish you wouldn't have said? Or maybe you took an illustration too far and were not at all planning to be as blunt as you were? Planning your words in advance can help save you from yourself sometimes.

One value of a sermon manuscript you may not think about is your material is then preserved in print. The legacy of information you will be able to leave the next generation may prove invaluable.

Both of my grandfathers were preachers. Grandpa McClintock was a Pentecostal preacher for decades. Papa Dodds was a Southern Baptist preacher for nearly fifty years. Upon their deaths, I was given books they had accumulated and binders filled with sermons they had created. I wish they had written out the sermons word for word instead of recording abbreviated outlines. I have enjoyed flipping through the binders and reading the notes, following their train of thought and enjoying the messages they had felt led by God to preach. I have personally found inspiration from some of those sermons and developed my own messages from their recorded thoughts.

"By writing and producing sermons in print, the instructional influence and ministry can be extended to a wider audience as . . . the great inspiration and instruction we receive by reading the preserved sermons of John Calvin, Martin Luther, John Wesley, George Whitefield, the Puritans, Jonathan Edwards and so many others of the past and present. When we realize the great influence these preachers had in people's lives in their own day and of the countless others through the years, we come to the conclusion that writing and preserving sermons has great value and ministry potential."[50]

To summarize, here are five good reasons to use a manuscript:

1. Clarity

When you take time to write the entire message out word for word, you are given the opportunity—well ahead of your delivery—to think through every word, idea, and concept. Sometimes what we think is clear in our minds is not so clear when we try to articulate it. This preparation process allows you time to clarify what you think you mean. Now you will be able to be more lucid, eloquent, and expressive with the way you communicate that particular point in your sermon.

2. Assurance

Let's just be honest: there is a lot of pressure on you to deliver something of value to the congregation every Sunday. Knowing exactly what you are going to say eases the nerves and gives you a sense of confidence. You are now free to step into the pulpit and deliver exactly what you were feeling during preparation. And once you grow in this method, you will have the liberty to step away from your script and speak extemporaneously at times because you know your message so well.

3. Succinctness

If you have not taken the time to carefully think through your thoughts and ideas, writing them out word for word, you may get to a point in your message and not communicate that point with completely accuracy. Instead, you will search and search for that right word to nail down that idea. Searching for the right way to say something only drags out your sermon.

That message becomes like the pilot who gets clearance to land but then keeps pulling back up deciding to circle the airport one more time. Audiences have a tough time putting up with ramblers and people who never get that plane landed.

4. Inspiration

Writing everything out instead of jotting down short thoughts in bullet form allows you to become a little more creative. This will hopefully permit you to craft better illustrations and applications. Also, your manuscript does not have to be formatted like a formal paper you would be writing for a professor. Instead, you will want to be a little more inventive and write for the ear and not for the eye. It is all about how it sounds to your audience— not how it looks on paper.

5. Momentum

As you sit down to write, one of the hardest things is simply getting started. But once you get started, it is easy to get on a roll. That momentum almost gives you a sense of being in front of your audience and sharing the excitement of the message you are creating. As you write and tweak, write and tweak, you are trying out each and every word, thought, and idea to an imaginary audience. You get to hear how you would say something and quickly know either "No. I need to say that a little differently." Or "Yes. That is really good, if I should say so myself."

INTERVIEW

KEN GURLEY

Below are comments taken from an interview with Ken Gurley, pastor of the First Church of Pearland (Pearland, Texas), on the topic of preaching from a manuscript:

Have you always manuscripted your sermons?

Yes, I've always written my sermons out word for word. When time length or messaging is crucial—such as in special services or meetings—my manuscript will be even more polished with time-frames, video or audio prompts, etc.

Who/What made the biggest impact on you developing this style?

The messages of J. T. Pugh probably impressed me more than any other in this area. Secondarily, reading the messages of G. H. Morrison and Clarence Macartney prompted me to do my sermons word for word.

Do you ever preach without a written manuscript?

I never go into a service without a manuscript sermon, yet when I feel impressed during the service to bid adieu to the full manuscript, I don't find it difficult to preach without one.

What do you see as the pros of preaching by a full manuscript?

This method of preparing messages permits me several advantages: a) Opportunity to look for holes in my logic and sequencing of points; b) Easier to gauge the time-length of the message; c) Keeps me on target in presenting my thoughts to the particular audience, especially when I'm weary; d) The preacher is more relaxed, knowing that he's done his "homework" and by being relaxed can more easily sense the Spirit's moving.

What do you see as the cons of preaching by a full manuscript?

The negatives of preaching by manuscript are fewer than the positives. Chief amongst the negatives, however, is the minister who preaches a manuscript sermon as if it is a book report. The language can be stilted and the audience can be easily distracted.

How do you prepare your manuscript?

After I've studied the Scriptures, marshaled my other Scriptures and possible illustrations, I mentally create the framework of the message from the beginning to ending. Once I've got a handle on the message, I begin writing the manuscript.

How do you deliver it in a way that doesn't sound like you are reading?

I find all that's needed with a well-prepared, manuscript message is to read over it several times prior to preaching. This allows my heart and mind to be filled with the message and, as Scripture says, from the abundance of the heart, the mouth speaks. I generally do not read a message but will use elements of the manuscript during transitions or when I'm needing to get a scriptural reference, historical point, statistic or a nuanced statement exactly right.

Who has made the biggest impact on you as a preacher?

The biggest impact made on my calling as a preacher is twofold. My mother was a teacher; my father was the preacher. My mother was a student of the Bible, and she taught in the Bible college in Jamaica; and many of the people she taught are now the leaders in the Jamaican Apostolic church (e.g., Sammy Stewart, Bobby Stewart, Devon Dawson, and Arthur Thomas). The success of their ministries, to a great extent, can be attributed to the Bible studies that my mom did in the Kingston church and the Bible school she taught in. Most nights she was up in her little 6' x 8' office, pecking with her index fingers on an old-fashioned Underwood typewriter. I have a huge binder of her notes on the Tabernacle plan that she taught. She drilled that into the minds and spirits and hearts of the Jamaicans. That is what has put them on a solid rock for even today's changing world. She was my model as a teacher, and my dad was my model as a preacher.

He preached fifteen to twenty minute sermons, gave altar calls, and people poured into the altar. It was incredible! But he only had a second grade education. He was born in 1900. God called him to preach—five months after he received the Holy Ghost—at the age of twenty-two. He went out on the back of a flatbed truck in Mississippi to preach to his home community under brush-arbors so his family would be saved. That church (Pleasant Ridge, Mississippi) still stands today because of that kind of preaching.

THE POWER
OF PERSONALITY
IN PREACHING

I praise you, for I am fearfully and wonderfully made.
Wonderful are your works; my soul knows it very well.
Psalm 139:14 (ESV)

We have all been uniquely made by God. Parts of our personalities are similar, but overall we are different and unique in our own right. The environments we have been raised in and the experiences we have had have all shaped us into the men and women we are today. Accepting the call to preach does not wipe the slate clean and cause us to start all over. No, the past has molded us, and each of us brings something different to the work God has called us to do.

Because of this important truth, we have a responsibility to be ourselves as we fulfill the call of God that rests upon our lives. Instead of saying too much myself in this chapter, I felt there were two people who could give us all a better understanding of how to fulfill the call to preach while remaining true to the person God has called them to be.

INTERVIEW

JEFF ARNOLD

Below are comments taken from an interview with Jeff Arnold, pastor of The Pentecostals of Gainesville (Gainesville, Florida), on the topic of the power of personality in preaching:

I have tried all these years to be me. And that has been my issue. I meet young preachers and they ask me, "What are your study habits? How do you do this? How do you do that?" I tell people it is really easy, "I am the best Jeff Arnold I know." I hear a lot of guys mimic me; but when they say "You dingbat and slob," it doesn't go over well. Because that is part of my "Brooklynese." I was brought up that way.

When I was coming up, I was just taught, "You need to be who you are, and you need to be honest and transparent." You can't believe all the preachers who have button-holed me and pulled me to the side and told me point blank, "You know, Arnold, you are just a little too honest in all this stuff. You really make it rough on the rest of us." I said, "Well, you ought to stop trying to be the pope. If you are a screwball, why don't you tell your audience, 'Hey I messed up. I made a mistake.' Why do you guys have to do this prima donna, Pentecostal image stuff? [They think,] "I got to protect my image."

I preached at a particular place, and I just poured my heart out. I was sobbing and crying. I told them, "I have shortcomings in my life. I try to overcome them. Sometimes I make a decision, and it blows up in my face; and I realize I went the wrong way about it and had to ask for forgiveness." Those preachers were mad at me about that. What in the world are you doing? You don't get up there and tell people you messed up. I said, "Why? Don't you mess up?" "Yes, but you don't tell the audience that." I said, "That's why you are just a fake. You are trying to maintain your image." I said, "I heard from the Lord that all He wants us to be is honest and transparent about our good points or our bad points."

I don't think you lose any confidence from the people when you are just trying to be open and honest. You don't have to make them believe you are always on top. Sometimes you are on the bottom of the manure pile.

I have always felt like Jesus has been so easy to live for and work for. All He has ever asked me to be is honest; honest when I win and honest when I lose. Be naked and transparent. Don't try to project some kind of image so that you are superior to people. And I guess I have always resented anything contrary to that. The only One who is superior is the Lord. The rest of us are just pieces of clay and dirt; trash that He recycled and put into His army and let us work for Him—that's all.

One of the best things that ever happened in my life took place when I was preaching for the prophet, T. W. Barnes. I was scared to death. I was a young preacher, and I preached from John 5 about the man at the pool of Bethesda. After the service (he always called me "boy"), he said, "Let me tell you something, Boy. There were some powerful gifts working in you tonight." And I'm thinking, "There was?" I didn't know anything about them. He said, "Boy, I could see when you were preaching about that man at Bethesda, you put yourself right in that pool. You were right there at the edge." I thought, that's exactly what I had done, and I do it all the time. I put myself in the picture. I try to feel what they were feeling. I try to sense what they were sensing. I do this because people are struggling with life and they are trying to get through it. And they don't need some prima donna putting out some Pentecostal baloney. They need somebody to turn around and say, "Been there. Done that. Got the t-shirt."

Have you always been comfortable being you?

Yes. Always. Here's why: cause I didn't have anything. I was a hell-raiser. I was a honky-tonker. I was a whoremonger. I'm an ex-jailbird. I've been a criminal, a crook. I robbed places. I was a bad boy. I was on my way to a divorce court when the Lord dealt with me during the night, woke me up, and put me under conviction. We weren't even going to church. My wife and I were on our way to getting a divorce, and the Lord dealt with me, and we went to this Baptist church. They told us we were saved. My wife said, "Saved?" She was raised in Fred Kinzie's church out of an orphanage. I didn't know anything about that at the time. She was raised Apostolic and was baptized although she had never received the Holy Ghost. She asked them, "Well, what about the Holy Ghost? I haven't started talking in tongues yet."

I have been thrown out of bars. I have been thrown out of hotels. This was the first time I was ever thrown out of a church. I was so embarrassed. I was humiliated. The preacher turned around and said, "Would you please escort this couple out of my sanctuary? They are disturbing my service."

And outside of being saved, that was the greatest moment in my life. If my wife hadn't been with me, I would've jumped out of the window and gone to get drunk. But I went in the back, and they started telling me that "No, people don't get the Holy Ghost and speak in tongues. That was only for the apostles." My wife said, "They are lying to you, Jeffrey. I've seen people get it." They were just laughing at us and were trying to give us Scriptures. My wife said, "You take me to an Apostolic Jesus' name Pentecostal church." I didn't know anything about that kind of church.

Here's my miracle: I walked into that little Pentecostal church. It had about seventy-five people. It had a lady preacher. People were buckin' and snortin' and bangin' tambourines. In my mind I'm thinking, *These poor people must think God is deaf. Everybody is screaming at the same time.* And all of a sudden, out of nowhere, this thing just fell on me. It came across my face. It went down my legs and came back up. I could feel this. I worked for the power company. We used to have to go in substations and the vibrations from the transformers would make the hair on your arms stand up because they were so full of energy and powerful.

I turned to my wife and asked her, "What is this?" She said, "What is what?" I said, "You don't feel that? We are staying here!" She said, "We are?" And here is the miracle: I told her, "Patti, this is the same stuff that woke me up out of my sleep."

That's why I guess God started me out believing in the supernatural. Because He came into my house. I was a drunk. I was a liar. And He just woke me up in the middle of the night and told me I needed to go to church and get my life right because I was out of time. I felt that same presence in that little church. When I got the baptism of the Holy Ghost it was the same presence again. I was so convinced. You didn't have to give me a sixteen-week Bible study. God supernaturally touched me, and I knew it was real.

What advice would you give a young preacher who hasn't yet learned to be themselves?

They need to pick up some good role models that they admire. They do not need to focus on becoming those role models. They have to just be themselves. They must find out what pleases God.

My highest priority is, "Lord, all I want to do is please You." I really think sometimes that this is a missing ingredient in the Pentecostal movement. We need to get back to saying, "I just want to please God. I want to please God in this service. I want to please God when I am with other people. And when I don't please God, I want to be able to admit that I messed up. I shouldn't have said that or thought that and I ask for forgiveness."

T. F. Tenney invited me to be the night speaker for the Louisiana camp meeting. That, to me was the highest thing you could go do except for the rapture. There wasn't anything higher. Well, I was terrified. I was just beginning my pastorate in Gainesville as a young guy, and I thought, "Louisiana camp meeting? You gotta be kidding me." So I wrote him a letter and I thanked him. I still have his letter of invite. I said, "Thank you. I am honored beyond words. But, Brother Tenney, I am not a camp meeting speaker. And I am sure that I am not capable of preaching Louisiana camp meeting with ten thousand people there at night. But thank you."

Well, he wrote me back and said, "Brother Jeffrey, if you don't want to come because you have previous engagements, then fine. But please do not insult me and these presbyters. Every section takes a vote on who they want to come speak at their camp meeting. And out of all the sections of our state, you got all the votes. So do not tell us that we don't know good preaching."

So I said, "Well, ok."

I've asked God many times, "Help me, Lord. I say some things that upset people sometimes, but I don't mean to. I just want to communicate truth and create faith in people's lives. Because if people don't get touched, don't get healed, blessed and saved, then they should've just gone to the bar where at least they would've enjoyed themselves." Really, that's the way my mindset was.

When I get ready to go, I'm expecting God to bless. I'm going to pray and study and do the best I can, and that's all I can do. I have done my utmost best to not think of myself more highly than I am.

Brother C. M. Becton corrected me one time. I was preaching at Brother Jones' church in St Louis. People were dancing. I preached the paint off the wall. People got the Holy Ghost. It was powerful. I made the statement, "I'm just a slob doing my job." I used to say that a lot. But after church, C. M. Becton button-holed me and he said, "Brother Arnold, that was the most fabulous message I have ever heard in my life." But he said, "I want to tell you something. Don't make reference to yourself by saying, you're just a slob, doing your job. You are a long way from being a slob."

That so impacted me. I knew he did that because he loved me. I took that to heart. And from that time until this day, I've never used that cliché again. I told the Lord, "You're right, Lord. I am not a slob. I'm a child of God. I've got my faults, but I'm a child of God."

I am thankful for people in my life who can speak into my life. Have some good people in your life who can speak into your life rather than someone who will tell you what you want to hear. That, I think is a disease in our movement. We hang around the same spiritual nincompoops who are as spiritual as a dead frog, and then they are going to tell us how great we did. We don't need that. I just need people in my life who will talk to me straight. I don't like it sometimes, but I need it. I look at it as a way of God saying to me, "You asked me to help you."

I was going through a very difficult time several years ago at Because of the Times. Lawsuits. People leaving the church left and right. I had done nothing wrong. I was devastated. I was in the motel room and was bawling my eyes out. I was praying, asking why all this was being done to me. I was ashamed and embarrassed. I felt like the Lord spoke to me. I heard these words in my mind. "I thought you said you wanted to be like Me." "Yes. I do, Lord." And He said, "Oh, you thought Me walking on the water, changing the water to wine, raising Lazarus from the dead. Oh, that's what you meant. Oh, I thought maybe like being cursed, being misunderstood, being talked bad about, being forced to live alone with your own commitments and your own values. That's what I was thinking about."

I try to tell people, "do not let your failures or your disappointments or your setbacks define you." Because you will become the man with the withered hand, the woman with the issue of blood, and blind Bartimaeus. All these people were defined by their messes. I see so many people whose successes and failures define them. They should be defined by the fact that they have peace with God and they are doing their best to please God.

INTERVIEW

CINDY MILLER

Below are comments taken from an interview with Cindy Miller, copastor of Calvary Tabernacle United Pentecostal Church (Wrightstown, New Jersey), on the topic of the power of personality in preaching:

How does someone find their voice (who they are) as a preacher?

In the beginning I was probably lost in all of that—finding my voice and who I was as a preacher. I was looking at how other people—both men and women—did it. But specifically as a woman, with very few role models, the few women I would see, I would watch closely how they would handle themselves in the pulpit. I would watch how they presented difficult topics. Because we don't preach like men. So I was trying to find my way with that; what that would even mean for me to preach. I would say, "I'm speaking or I'm teaching." To even come to the idea that I was preaching didn't come easy.

But as I moved through it—I think as I began to grow as a counselor—and I really figured out who I was as a person, who I was as a woman, and became very secure in who I was in Christ, that began to be heard in my messages. I approach the Scripture through a counselor's lens. It's almost like I can't help it. That's how I read. I'm always thinking from that angle. So in my messages I want people to be reflective. I try to stay in the Word, use the Scripture and walk them through, "What does this mean to you?"

My core conviction is the Word is powerful, it is truth, and it speaks. So early on, in watching people deliver messages, I knew I was really turned off by people who preached "books." It seemed like I saw that a lot. Instead of having the Word of

God, teaching me the Word of God, and leading me through the Word of God, it would be the latest book out and they were just kind of recycling its language. I knew I didn't want to be that kind of preacher. So maybe I started off finding my voice by figuring out what I didn't want to do. I would say, "That's not me. I don't like that. That's not true to who I am." Or "I don't agree with that." Figuring out what I didn't want to do helped me figure out what I did want to do.

Talk about that struggling to find "you" in the pulpit

Especially years ago, there were so few women in the pulpit. I guess the first women I knew that were preachers were Sister Vesta Mangun and Sister Nona Freeman. Then I met Sister Janet Trout and Sister Isabel Schweiger. They are all so extremely different. As I looked at them and was admiring them, I was intimidated by them. But success at that time was preaching like a man. Because if you are "preaching," that designated a man. A lot of times people would say, "Sister Nona Freeman will be *speaking* this morning and Brother Freeman will be *preaching* tonight." That was the language they would use.

So it took a long time for me to even consider myself a preacher. "I'm a preacher?" That was just so odd to me. I didn't even think of myself as that. I think that was part of the struggle. Knowing that I had this calling. Knowing I had this desire to bring God's Word and yet trying to find out how I was going to do that as a woman. I think it goes back to the fact that in my younger years I really didn't know who I was. I was insecure.

You're still trying to figure out who you are, trying to find your way in your twenties and early thirties. But the more comfortable I became with "who I am" just as a woman, then the more comfortable I could be finding my place in the pulpit. That's one reason I love aging. Because I don't have that struggle anymore. I know who I am. I appreciate what I bring. I feel like I do bring something different. And I don't worry about, "Are men going to accept me or not?" You know, I just feel like I am in a different place in life.

I have been honored to preach for all levels of ministry in different places. So I no longer bring my fear and intimidation into the room with me. I feel like I am here because I bring something unique to the pulpit. I have a unique approach and a unique way of presenting something, and they need my voice. They need what only I can bring. I'm not competing with a man. I don't want to compete with a man. I don't want to be a man. I don't want to be manly. I think I can be successful standing behind the pulpit without stomping, yelling, snorting, and spitting, and be effective.

Maybe all it took was for me to redefine preaching by asking myself, "What does preaching mean to me?" And when I redefined what preaching meant, then I could say, "Yes, that is something I can do." That helped me really get through the struggle.

How does one become comfortable in their own skin as a preacher and allow who they are to come through?

Early on, some of us, maybe not all of us, we are wanting to impress. I was not always thinking that consciously, but I wanted to impress the congregation. I wanted to impress the leadership. I wanted to impress God. And that would validate my calling. If they were all going "Wow!" then yeah, I am called. But then moving past that, and focusing on the end result, I would ask, "What do I want to happen?" The answer: I want to have influence. A lot of times when you impress people, they end up being intimidated by you. But when you stop that and instead you are trying to influence, that helps to bring down the walls and says to the people, "We are more alike than we are different. I don't have it all together."

That vulnerability is important. "Let me share my journey with you, because I have been where you are now." Or "Someday you may go down this path, and I wish someone had told me how they got to the end of it." I think being vulnerable, sharing my story, being willing to share my faults, the places I messed up, or where I didn't get it right is important.

I love humor. I love to laugh. And I think I want the congregation to connect with me emotionally through laughter as well as tears—if they are appropriate. But usually in my preaching there is a place to connect emotionally, not just through their thoughts; but I am trying to connect through their emotions. Anyone who knows me will tell you I love to laugh and that I will try to find something funny in everything. I think that is important. When people are laughing they are more open than at any other time. Defenses are down because "Oh, she is funny." And then in that moment, as their defenses are down, we are now on the same page. Then they will let me share something that is a little more difficult to absorb.

How much vulnerability is acceptable in the pulpit?

It's not confession. It's vulnerability. I've said to people in certain settings, "You know, the first five years of my marriage was horrible, and we probably both wished we could've gotten a divorce. But we were in ministry." That is shocking to people. To me, that's not shocking. That's a fact, and I am very comfortable with it. Because I know that's not where we are now. Then I proceed to say, "But God didn't leave us there." However, what I don't share is what was ugly about those five years. I can tell you it was ugly and tell you it was difficult. I can tell you there were ungodly moments with two people who were trying to live for God and work for God. But they don't need to hear about certain things.

I want to give them enough for them to know I understand. I want to give them enough that they know I am coming as someone who has actually experienced this wonderful healing journey. I think I would rather follow someone that I know has been there and is now here. I can follow that person as opposed to someone who never had a marriage problem or whatever. They've never had a down moment. They've never struggled in their faith. And they are kind of like, "I don't

249

know why you struggle. All of us have it together." I would just be intimidated by them.

Why can't you say, "I've struggled in my faith?" "What are you afraid of?"

What about things you are struggling with right then, in the present?

I think sometimes people need to sit down for a while when they are struggling because it leaks through their pores. There was one preacher I knew whose wife died and he was saying all the right things: "God is in control. God knows what he is doing." But he was so angry because he was in the middle of the grief cycle, and anger is part of it. He couldn't be angry at God, so he preached angry messages, rebuking people, and telling them they were all going to hell.

So I think when people have internal struggles, there are times when they need to sit down and not open their mouths for three months, six months, or whatever. In other areas, we just have to be mature and not abuse the church with our struggle.

In my opinion, being vulnerable when you are right in the middle of a struggle is not wise. Because, "I don't have the victory over it. I am not far enough past it to say the right thing." I think preaching is supposed to be leading people to a better place. But if I am stuck in the middle, I shouldn't be preaching about it because I don't know where to lead them. I'm not out of it yet. However, you do need to talk with someone before you implode or explode.

What advice would you give somebody who is trying to be like you?

There's only one me. I do think what happens is—because I travel and because there are very few women preachers—I get a lot of requests, "Oh, I want you to mentor me." Or I have people jokingly say, "When I grow up I want to be just like you." And I do tell them, "There is only one me, and you are not it. But there is only one you, and you need to fully be you. And I would love to help you fully be you." I think that language starts them thinking, *what does it mean to be fully me?*

I do not take someone on for mentoring and say, "I'm your mentor." Instead I say, "I would like to be part of your mentoring team." If you only have one mentor, I think it is more of a cloning thing going on. If that is all you know, you are going to only do things that way.

What is something a preacher (beginner or seasoned) can begin doing today that will improve their preaching?

It goes back to prayer. I remember a preacher telling me about being an assistant pastor and watching his pastor counsel people and continually tell them, "Well, you need to go pray about that." Then when he became a pastor, it all made sense in that it really is the answer to everything.

You can be deliberate in your prayers. You can pray, "Lord I want to preach more effectively. Help me to preach more effectively. And if that is not the right prayer to pray, help me to know the right prayer to pray. And help me to pray that prayer for the right reasons." I used to be scared to pray the wrong prayers. People have said, "Don't pray for humility." But I need humility. And if God doesn't give it to me, somebody else will; and they would do it in a way that may not be the best help to me. So I set those fears and worries aside a long time ago.

So pray and be honest with God and say the things you need and feel to say.

THE
ANOINTING

Jesus went to Nazareth, where he had been brought up, and on the Sabbath day he went into the synagogue, as was his custom. He stood up to read, and the scroll of the prophet Isaiah was handed to him. Unrolling it, he found the place where it is written: "The Spirit of the Lord is on me, because he has anointed me to proclaim good news to the poor. He has sent me to proclaim freedom for the prisoners and recovery of sight for the blind, to set the oppressed free, to proclaim the year of the Lord's favor" (Luke 4:16-19, NIV).

Some have made the anointing to be something mystical and incapable of being truly understood. It is like a butterfly flittering from place to place, and we can only hope it will stop and land on us. It is something so beautiful and wonderful; yet when you get close enough to recognize its existence, it flutters away, looking for another landing spot. There may be some truth to that. But for the most part, the anointing is something we can seek to understand more and more, embracing it as a marvelous gift from the Lord.

Jesus declared through a reading of Isaiah's prophecy that He was anointed to preach the gospel and deliver those who were bound in sin and sickness. The disciples who were gathered together in a prayer meeting proclaimed "How God anointed Jesus of Nazareth with the Holy Ghost and with power: who went about doing good, and healing all that were oppressed of the devil; for God was with him" (Acts 10:38). God had manifested Himself in flesh as Jesus Christ, to fulfill His holy work. The word "Christ" is the English transliteration of the Greek word *Christos* which means "the anointed one." Jesus was the Anointed One.

What Is the Anointing?

Though we can discuss and understand aspects of the anointing, we must realize that anything having to do with the Spirit of God is impossible for the human intellect to completely understand. God has revealed to us in His Word explanation and application of the anointing, yet the more we know about the anointing—and subsequently His Spirit—the more we realize we do not really know.

In a general sense, the anointing is a work of the Spirit of God. Oftentimes we will refer to someone by saying, "The hand of the Lord is on them." What we are saying is that we see something in their life that appears to be God's favor, God's calling, and God's purpose. What we are actually recognizing is the anointing of the Lord upon their life. What we are witnessing is God at work in their life to accomplish His will.

Anyone who has received the Holy Spirit is anointed. "But ye have an *unction* from the Holy One, and ye know all things . . . But the *anointing* which ye have received of him abideth in you, and ye need not that any man teach you: but as the same *anointing* teacheth you of all things, and is truth, and is no lie, and even as it hath taught you, ye shall abide in him" (I John 2:20, 27, emphasis mine).

"Unction," another word denoting anointing, is used to describe the act of anointing or being anointed. "Kings, prophets, and priests were anointed, in token of receiving divine grace. All believers are, in a secondary sense, what Christ was

254

in a primary sense, 'the Lord's anointed'" ("Unction," *Easton's Bible Dictionary*, 678).

Jesus said several things about the function of the Holy Spirit which we can also assume parallels the function of the anointing of that Spirit.

The Spirit will comfort us, teach us, and bring God's Word to our minds:

"These things have I spoken unto you, being yet present with you. But the Comforter, which is the Holy Ghost, whom the Father will send in my name, he shall teach you all things, and bring all things to your remembrance, whatsoever I have said unto you" (John 14:25-26).

The Spirit will guide us into all truth, reveal God's plan, and to glorify God:

"I have yet many things to say unto you, but ye cannot bear them now. Howbeit when he, the Spirit of truth, is come, he will guide you into all truth: for he shall not speak of himself; but whatsoever he shall hear, that shall he speak: and he will shew you things to come. He shall glorify me: for he shall receive of mine, and shall shew it unto you" (John 16:12-14).

The Spirit will give us power and make us witnesses:

"But ye shall receive power, after that the Holy Ghost is come upon you: and ye shall be witnesses unto me both in Jerusalem, and in all Judaea, and in Samaria, and unto the uttermost part of the earth" (Acts 1:8).

When we receive the Holy Ghost, we have these promises in our possession. In a sense, we have been anointed to experience and be filled with God's presence, God's purpose, God's plan, and God's power. As the *International Standard Bible Encyclopedia* states, we have been anointed for a "function or privilege." The preceding verses speak of both.

As a Spirit-filled child of God, you are anointed! God has placed His presence within you. His power rests upon your life. Yes, truly the "hand of God is upon you."

Though we may talk about different kinds of anointings and reasons for the anointing, what cannot be denied is that when we are anointed, it is always for a purpose. Jesus said He was anointed for at least five different reasons in Luke 4:16, though more reasons can be found throughout the New Testament.

Three Purposes of the Anointing

1. To set apart, to distinguish

When the Tabernacle's construction was complete with every article for Tabernacle service successfully created, God gave Moses specific instructions on what to do next:

"Then you shall take the anointing oil and anoint the tabernacle and all that is in it, and consecrate it and all its furniture, so that it may become holy. You shall also anoint the altar of burnt offering and all its utensils, and consecrate the altar, so that the altar may become most holy. You shall also anoint the basin and its stand, and consecrate it" (Exodus 40:9-11, ESV).

Merriam-Webster defines *consecrate* as "dedicated to a sacred purpose." God told Moses to pour oil over everything in the Tabernacle. Each piece of furniture was to be distinguished as more than ordinary furniture. These articles were to be set apart for worship and service unto the Lord.

The same thing happened with you and me when God's Spirit filled our lives. We were filled with God's holiness (Holy Spirit) and were dedicated to a sacred purpose. Paul appealed to the Roman believers on the basis of what God had done in their lives and for the purpose for which they had been saved: "I beseech you therefore, brethren, by the mercies of God, that ye present your bodies a living sacrifice, holy, acceptable unto God, which is your reasonable service. And be not conformed to this world: but be ye transformed by the renewing of your mind, that ye may prove what is that good, and acceptable, and perfect, will of God" (Romans 12:1-2).

The anointing that rests upon the lives of believers is present so that we may fulfill God's purpose in the world. This is the purpose of all who have been filled with God's Spirit—anointed.

2. To do something specific, for a function or privilege

Though there is a general anointing all believers receive when filled with the Holy Spirit, there are also specific anointings for specific callings.

"And thou shalt bring Aaron and his sons unto the door of the tabernacle of the congregation, and wash them with water. And thou shalt put upon Aaron the holy garments, and anoint him, and sanctify him; that he may minister unto me in the priest's office" (Exodus 40:12-13).

Under the Old Covenant, the priest was the individual given the responsibility of offering sacrifices for the people, and serving the Lord daily in the Tabernacle. This calling was signified by a ceremony where the priest was anointed with oil. This anointing was specific to this particular office. God had designated Moses to lead the Israelites out of Egypt, but Aaron and his sons were anointed to fill this specific priestly role in the community of God's people.

In later years, the children of Israel asked for a king. Though this was not God's plan, He did give them what they asked; but only on His terms. This king would be designated by God alone, and anointed.

"Then Samuel took a flask of olive oil and poured it on Saul's head and kissed him, saying, "Has not the Lord anointed you ruler over his inheritance?" (I Samuel 10:1).

Saul was anointed Israel's first king. As Samuel poured oil over his head, the significance of the event could not be denied. At that moment, Saul was being set apart and distinguished above all others in the kingdom. And this anointing was for a specific purpose and calling. This anointing was God's favor on Saul's life to rule as king of Israel.

Again, Luke 4:18 records Jesus stating that He was anointed for a specific purpose. And the first purpose He mentioned was, "to preach the gospel."

3. To preach the gospel

Just as there are specific anointings for specific callings, there are specific anointings for specific purposes.

Preachers gifted with tremendous communications skills can find themselves relying on their own abilities and seldom feeling a need for the anointing. In fact, you don't really need the anointing to preach. I know that sounds disrespectful and sacrilegious, but it is true. It doesn't take any special unction to speak what is found in the Bible. However, if you want to be more than an entertainer; if you want to be more than a motivational speaker who calls himself a preacher, then you must have the anointing.

If God calls you to preach, He gives you an anointing to fulfill that call. You can choose to operate under that anointing or not. The anointing is dependent upon at least four things:

1. The sovereignty of God

God chooses whom He will call and anoint. You do not choose to preach and receive the anointing to preach solely by your own volition. This is a sovereign work of God. Additionally, you do not control the anointing. You choose to submit yourself to the sovereign working of the Spirit or refuse to allow the Spirit free flow in your life.

2. Presence of a need

God knows who will be present to hear you preach. He also knows the needs they will be carrying with them. There may be addictions and sicknesses present in that service. But no matter the situation, God has the power to meet each need. It is difficult to explain how it happens, but when God's presence and power begin to minister, lives are changed. And they are often changed because of the anointing at work in a message being preached or a prayer being prayed.

3. Conductivity of the preacher

God never forces the Spirit's anointing on anyone. He will never forcefully "possess" someone and make them do

His will. You will never find yourself unexpectedly overtaken by the anointing as it interrupts your selfish plans to pursue your own desires. The anointing will only freely flow through someone who allows themselves to be a channel of God's choosing.

Why do some seem more anointed than others? First of all, perhaps what you are seeing is a small sample of someone's life. When you see them they may be always operating in the same specific call and it is a call God has specifically anointed them to fulfill. It does not necessarily mean they are more anointed than you or anyone else. But perhaps they have found that "sweet spot" of God's call in their life and have fully surrendered to it.

However, another possibility is some are more surrendered than others. There are several things that can increase the flow of the anointing while there are other things that will likely impede the flow.

Surrender, humility, penitence, boldness, and willingness are all attributes of someone who has learned to give themselves to the operation of the anointing in their lives. One must realize that God has to be in control. You and I need to surrender control. Though John was not talking about the anointing, his words still paint a great picture of surrender: "He must increase but I must decrease" (John 3:30).

An anointed preacher is humble. On the other hand, pride can destroy the anointing in someone's life. An anointed preacher is willing—willing to obey the Lord and do what He asks. This takes faith because sometimes what God asks will not make sense to your human mind. Yet, God's ways are above and beyond our ways, and He does know what is best. He sees into the realm of the eternal and knows what is at work in that individual's life that you may not be able to see.

An anointed preacher is bold. Oftentimes we miss out on moments of great anointing and miracles because we lack the boldness to act. It took boldness for Peter and John to look at a lame man who had been sitting for many years at the Temple gate and tell him to rise to his feet. Of course, there is also an aspect of God's will that must align with our boldness in order for the anointing to produce the results we desire. I know this may also sound sacrilegious, but it may not be God's perfect will for someone who is lame to walk. Therefore to simply go up to every lame person and tell them to "Get up and walk" would not be wise. Even Jesus didn't heal everyone He came in contact with. Remember His visit to His hometown? However, there are those moments when God does want to heal or deliver; and we, out of fear of humiliation refuse to step out in boldness and pray the prayer of faith over that individual. I have no doubt I have missed moments when God had anointed me for a purpose I didn't fully understand.

Of course, there are times when the anointing seems to operate in an unexpected way. Have you ever talked with someone and as you spoke, you felt differently than you normally do in everyday conversations? In fact, what began to flow out of your mouth were thoughts and ideas you had not previously prepared to say. Truly, the Holy Spirit was directing your thoughts and dictating the words proceeding from your lips. In many ways, you are operating in a specific anointing for that specific moment.

This can happen quite often while preaching under the anointing of the Holy Ghost.

4. Receptivity of the hearers

Have you ever preached and were confident that what you were saying was from God? In fact, while you were speaking you had no doubt God's anointing was resting upon you. However, the audience was unmoved, non-responsive, and uninterested in the word you had from the Lord. We have to remember, just as the anointing will not overtake you as a preacher who is not surrendered or open to what God wants to do through you, neither will God's power overtake someone who is sitting under the sound of your voice, refusing to give themselves to the admonitions coming across the pulpit. The Spirit will knock and make invitation for them to respond, but He will never beat the door down and storm their house.

"Behold, I stand at the door and knock. If anyone hears my voice and opens the door, I will come in to him and eat with him, and he with me" (Revelation 3:20, ESV).

One of the most important things to understand about the anointing is that God gives it for a purpose. There is a reason God has anointed you. And if you have received the anointing to preach the gospel, there is a reason for that.

We need to understand our role as preachers. We need to know who we are and what we are. We have been ordained and gifted by God to preach. God's sacred call went forth and arrested our souls. We have willingly bowed before His presence and surrendered to that call. To live in that anointing we must remain humble. We are no better than anyone else. In fact, we are called to serve others by studying, praying, and sharing the unfailing love of Christ with them.

Because of our calling and anointing, we cannot allow ourselves to do less than our best. Someone might say, "I don't really have to study or do a whole lot of work at preaching because I just rely on the Holy Ghost to anoint me when I get in the pulpit." The problem with that mindset is that this preacher seems to have forgotten Paul's command to Timothy: "Study to shew thyself approved unto God, a workman that needeth not to be ashamed, rightly dividing the word of truth" (II Timothy 2:15).

The *New Living Translation* says it this way: "Work hard so you can present yourself to God and receive his approval. Be a good worker, one who does not need to be ashamed and who correctly explains the word of truth."

I want to trust in God's anointing, but I also want God's approval. In fact, if I don't have God's approval, will I continue to have God's anointing?

Because we have been called and anointed we must rely on God to work. We are required to do our part, but ultimately it must be God who works in and through us for His will to be accomplished. We should study to show ourselves approved and then surrender all of our efforts to Him. When we do our part, we can be confident God will do His.

Because we have been called and anointed, we must leave the results to God. When you preach under the anointing of the Holy Ghost as a completely surrendered man or woman of God, the results are up to Him. No matter what happens when you preach, you do not get to take the credit for any outstanding results, nor do you get to take the blame for a lack of results. If someone is healed or saved, God gets the glory. If no one responded, and it appears no one was saved, God gets the glory. The results are all left to Him.

What are three things a preacher (beginner or seasoned) can begin doing today that will improve their preaching?

Study preaching. When you listen to people, learn by their successes and mistakes. When I hear someone who has a distracting mannerism, I will ask my wife, "Do I do anything that distracts people?" Be a good listener and observer.

You must read every day. The preachers that read are the most interesting to listen to. You can tell if they read or not. If you don't read, you will just keep rewinding the same old sermons and will become boring and predictable. This is especially true when you fill the same pulpit week after week. You have to be a reader and keep filling your well up.

Prayer. You cannot be a successful communicator with a consistent anointing with a quick hop in the prayer room just a few minutes before you preach.

V

CONCLUSION

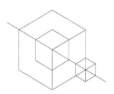

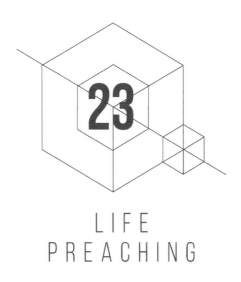

LIFE
PREACHING

Great preachers are not born, they are made.

D. Martyn Lloyd-Jones made the opposite statement: "Preachers are born, not made."[51] I believe Lloyd-Jones and I are saying much the same thing, just in a different way.

Through the years, I have had the wonderful privilege of sitting under the sound of hundreds of men and women as they delivered burdens through the vehicle of preaching. Some screamed and yelled until their face turned red and their clothes were soaked. Others calmly stood behind the pulpit and spoke without struggle or strain. I have been greatly impacted when the volume was high. I have been greatly impacted when the volume was low. I have witnessed conviction compel people to repent at the end of an eloquent message, and I have witnessed similar conviction confront people when the message was not so eloquent.

I am convinced great preaching is more than style, volume, eloquence, or even well-organized content. The greatest preaching comes from a life that has experienced the power, presence, and Person of Jesus Christ. I am not discounting the importance of studying to "shew thyself approved," because this entire book has stressed the importance of preparation. However, I am seeking to draw attention to the one side of preaching that, if ignored, causes the gospel to be of no effect: God taking a man or woman with a calling and making them a preacher.

A man can know how to exegete Scripture, but not know how to preach.

A woman can know how to string sentences together, but not know how to preach.

Paul said, "My message and my preaching were not accompanied by clever, wise words, but by a display of the Spirit's power" (I Corinthians 2:4, ISV). Yes, great preaching must have a biblical foundation, but great preaching must also be real. End-time pulpits do not need to be filled with prima donnas. Hurting people do not need cocky preachers postulating about how they have their life together and never face struggle. Preachers who think they live a holy life largely free of troubles do not have the right to talk down to me like I am lost and have travelled beyond the love and grace of God.

I want to look at these preachers and tell them, "Come on! Just be real. You battle fear just like me. Admit it. That admission may help you better connect with your audience. You fail and make mistakes just like everyone else. You gossip sometimes. You are judgmental sometimes. You lack grace and compassion sometimes. You fail to please God sometimes. Admit it! Let your broken and contrite heart be revealed to the people to whom you are preaching. Yes, they need to know they can be overcomers, but what about you? Why not share some of the struggles you have overcome?"

Great preaching is transparent. I am not saying you should hang out all your dirty laundry every Sunday for the church to see. That would not be wise. But it is all right to let people see behind the facade. In fact, what people really need is for their preacher to be so transparent that Jesus is seen through them. You must be relatable. Don't live on a pedestal. That is not your calling. Your calling is to be a preacher, a servant, and a man or woman conveying God's love to the world.

Great preaching comes through the filter of experience; experience that is validated by the truth of the Bible. Again, "Great preachers are not born, they are made." Here is why I say this:

Great preaching grants grace because the preacher personally understands the depths of God's sufficient grace. There are a variety of circumstances they can point to illustrating God's endless grace. They realize their unworthiness because of their unfaithfulness. Yet they recognize their privilege because of God's power revealed in their life. Their preaching oozes with grace. Their words are weighed with kindness as they carefully communicate God's gifts available to those who will come to Him.

Great preaching communicates compassion because the preacher has personally experienced the mercy and compassion of Christ. They remember aimlessly wandering without hope and are convinced it was Christ's compassion that rescued them. They cannot forget the moment Jesus found them. They keep the memory of that experience close, vowing to live life in such a way that tells the Lord, "Thank You!"

Great preaching proclaims power because the preacher has personally witnessed the power of God at work in his or her own life. Whether it was healing or deliverance miraculously wrought in his or her own life or the lives of loved ones, the preacher emphatically declares the availability of God's mighty power. He or she understands the reality of God's power because of personal revelation and experience.

Great preaching testifies to transformation because the preacher has personally discovered the reality of old things being passed away and all things becoming new. He remembers his old life and the dangerous path he once travelled.

He can never fully remove from his mind the lifestyle of the past. But those memories only fuel his passion to testify to the world. He testifies that those who will turn to Jesus can receive the Holy Spirit and know the power of transformation for themselves.

Great preaching promises hope because the preacher personally knows both the depths of discouragement and the assurance of faith. The preacher regularly draws from the well of wisdom recounting the moments he almost gave up only to recognize the presence of the "ever-present help in trouble" (Psalm 46:1, NIV). He speaks to those in the valley, helping to lift their eyes to the mountain. He calls to those on the stormy sea to look for Jesus in the belly of their boat. As he preaches, he highlights hope, uncovers faith, and emboldens expectancy for the never-failing promises of God.

After Peter and John had come to Samaria and prayed for the believers to receive the Holy Ghost, Simon tried to get them to sell this ability. He was enamored by the signs that followed these two preachers of the gospel. There are so-called preachers who desire the effects and impact of preaching that result from true preachers of the gospel. They figure there must be an easy way to attain that ability and power.

What Simon failed to realize was that true preaching, life preaching, takes place from a place of transformation. Only those who have been changed by the gospel have the ability to effectively preach the gospel. Preach from a place of transformation and watch the Holy Ghost change lives.

Look at the seven sons of Sceva in Acts 19. They went around trying to cast out demons, imitating what Paul had been doing under the anointing of the Holy Ghost. They were eventually exposed. An evil spirit spoke to them, "Jesus I know, and Paul I know about, but who are you?" (Acts 19:15, NIV). The enemy recognizes true preachers of the gospel.

The impact of your preaching will be determined by the depth of your relationship with Jesus Christ. You can only effectively preach Jesus if you know Jesus.

You cannot preach what you do not know. You can preach *about* it, but you cannot preach it. A preacher can talk about a relationship with God, but without experience it is merely supposition based on hearsay. You cannot preach with assurance and conviction what you have not experienced for yourself. I believe we can preach many things by faith, but experience brings greater persuasion and conviction. Just as you cannot preach the meaning of Matthew 16:18 without knowing its context, you cannot preach the comfort found in pain, if you have not known pain. A preacher cannot truly preach miracles if he has not known what it is to need one.

This is the difference between preaching head-to-head or heart-to-heart. Both need attention. Both need to be transformed. But what is in the heart, not the mind, determines the actions of our lives. As a man "thinks in his heart, so is he" (Proverbs 23:7, NKJV).

As a preacher, your greatest preaching will be born out of your greatest adversities. Hours of research will likely produce great content. But your most profound messages will be fashioned on the battlefield and shaped in the storm.

As a preacher, your greatest messages will be born in the valleys of life. They will be sound interpretations of Scripture because of your study, but they will be moving and compassionate because of the darkness you stumbled through.

As a preacher, your greatest messages will be developed on the mountain. They will have depth of Bible knowledge because of your expertise and training, but they will challenge the listeners because of the intense climb you had to make to reach the top.

People will come to church and honor you as pastor because they know you are an expert in the Scriptures. They will listen to you because you have lived a life that exemplifies those Scriptures.

Your church needs a preacher who will preach to them from a life that really knows the Savior. They must hear from a man or woman who has tasted of His presence and knows how to approach His throne. They want to hear from someone who has faced giants and lived to tell about it. They are looking for voices who have confessed faith in the face of doubt. This world needs preachers who will preach righteousness out of experience and compassion, not theory and control. This world needs preachers who will declare God's power, God's love, and God's grace because they themselves have firsthand knowledge of each.

Do you desire to be a better preacher? Then become a better "pray-er."

Do you desire to deliver better sermons? Then grip tightly to God's hand and face the battle head-on.

Read. Study. Prepare. Then let God mold your heart, renew your mind, and empower you to preach the Author of life through life preaching.

> *Some people ask me, "How long did*
> *it take you to prepare that sermon"?*
> *I tell them, "sixty-three years."*
>
> —*T. F. Tenney*

VI

APPENDIXES

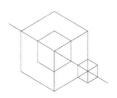

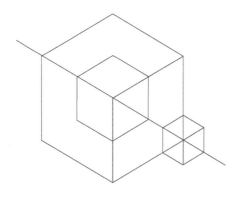

APPENDIX 1
THE PHYSICAL SIDE OF
PASSION IN PREACHING

INTERVIEW
WITH

JERRY JONES

Below are comments taken from an interview with Jerry Jones, general secretary of the United Pentecostal Church International, on the topic of the physical side of passion in preaching:

The passion is not physical all the time. It expresses itself physically, but the passion you feel for what you're doing is an internal thing; and it expresses itself in word choice, sentence syntax, cadence, rhythm, the flow of the points . . .

passion is more than the physical side. If you feel passion, there will be a physical manifestation of that passion. You cannot help that, but passion is deeper and greater than that. Like I said, it reveals itself in other ways.

The physical side then is a reaction to three things in my opinion. It is a reaction to the passion you feel, the anointing that is on you, and the response the crowd is giving you. The anointing is supernatural. You do not control the anointing. You can create an atmosphere that is conducive to the anointing both in your private life, and in your preparation for the sermon by really mastering the material. This will allow you to be free rather than locked into an unfamiliar progression of points. All these things can free you up so the anointing flows. But it is supernatural. It is God's part.

The other things: the reaction you feel to the crowd getting with you (the size of the crowd, the importance of the meeting make a difference—i.e. a Wednesday night Bible study at your home church and you have done a thousand of them—probably your physical reaction will be lessened . . . but stand before a general conference and your emotion rises) is all physical. That's human. That is not God. It's not bad. It's us.

Then your own passion for what you're preaching and maybe the emotion you feel when you look out in the crowd and see people whose lives are obviously in disarray. They need help. There's a human element. Jesus looked at the crowd, and he felt compassion. That was the "Jesus" side. That was the human side. He had compassion on them. God is compassionate always. He doesn't have to look out at the crowd to be compassionate, but we do. And so, we have to be careful and understand then that the physical side of preaching, outside the anointing (if you will), is controllable. Since it's human, "the spirit of the prophet is subject to the prophet." And all I mean by that is, "you must handle that emotion and that passion." Even the techniques, like I mentioned before—leaving the pulpit, going out in the crowd, grabbing somebody's hand, and patting a kid on the shoulder—are controllable ultimately.

That brings us to the voice. Obviously volume modulation is a very important part of what we do. That's why sound people can kill a good sermon. Because when he or she tries to anticipate and control the amplitude of your voice, they're taking away a very important part of communication. If I can't get above the crowd when they're responding, if I can't get louder to emphasize a point, if I can't drop my voice to pull their attention back in, I'm crippled. So a sound man who turns you up when you drop your voice, turns you down when you raise your voice—or the bane of all verbal communication: the "automatic squelcher"—the compressor—puts you within a predetermined range of volume. That is a nightmare for any preacher because these are tools you use.

Abusing the Voice

Now, abusing the voice is something that can happen. I once pastored a speech therapist, and she helped me a lot. I'm not saying I have all the answers. I'm certainly not a doctor. But you speak from your diaphragm, not from your throat. If you speak from your throat, you will wear out your voice. If you project from your diaphragm, you are pushing the volume of air across the vocal cords, creating the volume, not creating the volume by further strain on those vocal cords to make that volume. You can sense this if you practice it. And I know that we live in an era where you are supposed to be natural. We even went through a period—thank the good Lord we are moving out of that period—where we are just supposed to sit there. And it is almost like—I hate to say it—we get this from religious television programs where people are just sitting there, and it's not churchy, and we eschew the old "platform." But the truth is, the reason why the old speakers like Lincoln could be heard by ten thousand people with no microphone, was that he did declaim and project. They projected by speaking from the diaphragm.

When you get through preaching, if you're not sore just below your ribcage; but instead you are sore just below your jaw line, you're not preaching from your diaphragm. And you need to learn to push harder—push the air across. The more air moving across your vocal cords, the less strain you place on the vocal cords to achieve volume or modulation of the voice. You must push the air across and that comes from the diaphragm, from deep breaths, from learning some of the breathing controls that singers use, and that comes with practice. It comes with a conscious decision to do that. That is the only way I know to protect your voice other than some tricks that some use: don't drink cold water immediately before or after preaching; be very careful about throat lozenges. And face the facts: just as any other physical difference can be, a person can just have a weak voice and has to learn to modulate and project to the limits or to the extent that their voice will allow.

A final comment on this: if you experience continual weakness and hoarseness, you should have someone check your vocal cords. You can get polyps or calluses on the vocal cords. You can get help by having these polyps or calluses removed. It's a scary thought. I've never lost my voice from preaching. I lose my voice when I haven't preached in a while. Somehow preaching keeps it strengthened. I've had it examined by doctors and have never found a polyp, callus, or any problems with my voice. I know I'm blessed. But early on I learned to preach from my gut rather than my throat.

How can we stay in control and use our voice to emphasize the message?

First of all, the awareness of it is half the battle. Knowing that you have a tendency toward that [losing control] will help you over time, as you preach; you can begin to feel that you are doing that. Sometimes the issue can still arrive—getting in a high pitch rhythm, it's almost a monotone, though it's not monotone because it is way up there. You can find yourself getting hung up in the high-passion, higher volume, and higher pitch, and it's hard to come back down. The best thing is not to get there, but to use cadence and rhythm in word choice, in pausing, etc., even when you're passionate. I think one good technique is to find a point, get to that point and stop. Just stop. Make a statement and just stop. Don't lose your crowd, don't turn away, but discover that there is greater emphasis made sometimes in a pause than in continuing on.

Another technique to use when you feel yourself reaching this point is to stop and have the audience praise God. Just stop. Bring the sermon to a stop. And begin to physically pull yourself back under control. This is the secret to powerful preaching within the confines of our physical limitations.

I often think about and read to myself sections of the "I Have a Dream" speech Dr. King gave. It's not really a speech. It's an old Baptist preacher's sermon. When Martin Luther King burst on the scene, his speaking was so captivating. Like Lincoln, Roosevelt, and Churchill; they were all passionate speakers. What Dr. King had that came through in front of the Lincoln Memorial was the cadences of an African American Southern Baptist Preacher. The rhythms that in a church service got "Amens" and rhythmic response from the crowd, the country at large had not been exposed to very much. So he was instantly hailed as a great speaker, and he was. But he was a preacher, and that's what people forget.

When you look at how his voice would rise on "a day when black children and white children would play together" and he would rise to this crescendo of words and then say, "I have a dream." Well, there was a pulling, a drawing in of the crowd. He was animated. You often miss it if you only hear the audio. But as he spoke, he had to stay at the mic because he had a couple hundred thousand people listening to him. But he was animated, and he moved; but the passion was very controlled, very rhythmically applied, and of course the well-chosen words that created the eloquence of it: "I Have a Dream" was in my mind a model of controlled human passion that was targeted and aimed at the end result. Almost like an arrow at a target, it didn't waiver.

There was an incredible level of passion. There was an incredible level of human energy in that speech and its delivery. But it was tightly controlled. There was nothing out of control about it. Again, that was a speech, and we can't claim any God-given anointing necessarily. But when you add the

279

factor of the anointing and learn to channel our reaction to the anointing and the crowd's response, our passion for what we are saying and trying to accomplish, and our compassion for those who are hearing us, it makes for a powerful delivery. That comes with experience.

I have watched young preachers sometimes who have mannerisms and distractions in the way they project things. I understand over time that they will learn how to eliminate the distractions. For some preachers, kids are out there counting how many times the preacher is saying "hallelujah" or "praise God." These "crutches" are mainly the result of inexperience. This is also because they are having trouble getting a handle on the human emotions, energy, and passion.

Sometimes the anointing has been so heavy on me, I confess, I had no control. The crowd was flowing with the emotion of the anointing, and I was caught up; and words came to me—phraseology, syntaxes, and rhythmic cadences of words I didn't anticipate—that weren't written. And people would come to me later and ask, "Can I have a copy of that?" Well, there is no copy of that. And we've all been there. And of course, that's so rare; we all remember when we were there. But I think a younger preacher without experience can easily detract from those moments because they're not as much in control and do not quite understand how it can be facilitated.

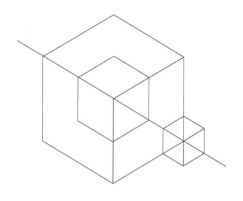

APPENDIX 2
THE DIFFERENCE BETWEEN
TEACHING AND PREACHING

You may have heard it said, "Preaching is yelling. Teaching is telling." Some individuals who may not be very emotional in the pulpit might say, "I'm really more of a teacher than a preacher." And then some grip the pulpit tightly, yell for thirty minutes about nothing in particular, and think they really preached. If we try to define preaching and teaching by merely focusing on noise level and emotion, we are completely missing the boat. These ideas come from a modern understanding of preaching and teaching instead of a biblical one. While I do not profess to be able to provide the definitive word on such a controversial topic, I would like to provide a brief review from a biblical perspective.

Let's first look at how biblical preaching and teaching are the same.

1. Passion should be a part of your message whether you are preaching or teaching.

Whether we are looking at Peter standing on the balcony of the upper room, preaching to the people in the streets, declaring the gospel message, or we are reading the words of Paul as he teaches the Galatians about the danger of turning away from the true gospel for a false one in Galatians chapter one, there is passion.

Passion is simply the depth to which you feel about something. It is made visible through many bodily expressions. Yes, it can come through in the raising of the voice or it can be witnessed in the way you look at someone. A hand gesture or the tone in which you express your words—these are all ways in which passion is portrayed. But the level of passion has nothing to do with whether or not you are teaching or preaching. You should be passionate in either case.

Believe it or not, it is possible to raise your voice and still be teaching. On the other hand, you can whisper a dramatic point and be preaching. You can wave your arms frantically, trying to get your point across and be teaching. Whereas, you can use a soothing tone of voice and be preaching.

2. Both should center on the gospel and the truth of God's Word.

The message being communicated should be the same. We are called to preach and teach the gospel. We are called to share Jesus Christ with the world. We share Him by showing love to one another, but we also share Him through teaching and preaching. Whether you are developing a lesson to teach, with the intent of building people's faith or instructing them how to live their lives in a way that is pleasing to the Lord, the foundation of that lesson must be the gospel and the Word of God. If you are preparing a sermon to preach, in order to stir those who are needing the Lord to turn to Him, then you must make sure the focus of that sermon points to Jesus Christ and the truth of the gospel.

You can take your text from Acts 2:38 or John 3:5 and be teaching. You can take your text from Deuteronomy 6:4 or John 1:1 and be preaching. The message will always be the same—the gospel, the truth of God's Word—but the focus of the message will be different.

Now, let's take a look at how biblical preaching and teaching are different.

As we discussed in chapter 1, preaching means "to herald, to announce, to proclaim." Biblical preaching is the pronouncement of the good news, the gospel. It is declaring to people something they may not already know. It then lays the foundation for teaching.

Teaching instructs, explains, and shows us how to live our lives in response to the good news.

"Whereas the message preached was the message announced, the message taught was the message explained, clarified, and applied, with exhortation to live by it. Whereas the message preached (announced) was primarily for the purpose of conversion, the message taught (explained, clarified, applied, with exhortation) was primarily for the purpose of building faith, Christian conviction and character."[52]

Preaching is announcing. Teaching is explaining.

The New Testament tells of the disciples both preaching and teaching. The pattern often takes the form of preaching first, then teaching. Therefore, preaching becomes the foundation and forerunner to teaching.

Matthew records the final words of Jesus in this manner:

"Go ye therefore, and teach all nations, baptizing them in the name of the Father, and of the Son, and of the Holy Ghost: Teaching them to observe all things whatsoever I have commanded you: and, lo, I am with you alway, even unto the end of the world. Amen" (Matthew 28:19-20).

Mark records what we assume to be the same account in this way:

"And he said unto them, Go ye into all the world, and preach the gospel to every creature" (Mark 16:15).

Jesus commanded His disciples to go everywhere and preach to everyone—to declare and proclaim the good news of the gospel. Announce to the world what Christ accomplished on the cross and let them know salvation is available for them. Then they were to teach those who responded to the gospel message. They were to explain how to live as believers. They were to show them how to apply the truth of the gospel to their lives and live out their faith in their everyday lives.

It was said of Paul in Acts 28, that he went about "Preaching the kingdom of God, and teaching those things which concern the Lord Jesus Christ, with all confidence, no man forbidding him" (Acts 28:31). This idea of "preaching the kingdom of God" brings to my mind what both John the Baptist and Jesus Christ both preached during their earthly ministries: "Repent, for the kingdom of heaven is at hand."

Thus, it appears that their preaching was a declarative message; a heralding of a command the hearers had not heard before, or had not heard in a while. Therefore, after Paul had preached to them, he then took time to teach them how to apply this truth and experience to their daily lives.

Look now at Paul's words to the Colossians:

"Whom we preach, warning every man, and teaching every man in all wisdom; that we may present every man perfect in Christ Jesus" (Colossians 1:28). There is first a heralding and proclaiming. Then comes the need for teaching. Preaching is announcing. Teaching is explaining.

"The pattern is consistent—preaching (making announcement) precedes teaching (explanation, clarification, application, exhortation). In any case, preaching and teaching go together. He who preaches (announces to the unconverted) also generally teaches (explains, clarifies, applies, and exhorts those who are already familiar with what has already been announced).[53]

Perhaps with this understanding, we may conclude that the majority of sermons we preach on a weekly basis have moments of both preaching and teaching. We may proclaim and announce certain aspects of the gospel, encouraging people to "hear the Word of the Lord," while at other points we are explaining, clarifying, and applying the truth we have just proclaimed.

What cannot be denied is we need both. So instead of being afraid of one or the other, we should recommit ourselves to engage in the practice of both with passion and purpose.

VII
REFERENCES

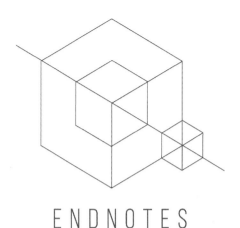

ENDNOTES

[1] Calvin Miller, *Preaching: The Art of Narrative Exposition* (Grand Rapids, MI: Baker Books, 2006), 41-42.

[2] John Piper, "Advice to Pastors: Preach the Word," February 5, 1996, *http://www.desiringgod.org/resource-library/sermons/advice-to-pastors-preach-the-word* (accessed May 29, 2015). See also Appendix 2 – "The Difference Between Teaching and Preaching."

[3] Calvin Miller, *Preaching*, 17.

[4] Mark Dever and Greg Gilbert, *Preach: Theology Meets Practice* (Nashville, TN: B & H Books, 2012), 21.

[5] Dever and Gilbert, *Preach*, 22.

[6] Dever and Gilbert, *Preach*, 51.

[7] Dever and Gilbert, *Preach*, 53.

[8] Dever and Gilbert, *Preach*, 53.

[9] Dever and Gilbert, *Preach*, 54.

[10] Kenton C. Anderson, Choosing to Preach: A Comprehensive Introduction to Sermon Options and Structures (Kindle ed; Grand Rapids, MI.: Zondervan, 2006), 401.

[11] Dever and Gilbert, *Preach*, 19.

[12] Dever and Gilbert, *Preach*, 30.

[13] Dever and Gilbert, *Preach*, 31.

[14] Dever and Gilbert, *Preach*, 50.

[15] J. Mark Hollingsworth, "Called to Preach," accessed May 29, 2015, *http://www.preachology.com/called-to-preach.html*.

[16] J. Mark Hollingsworth, "Divine Call to Preach or Man's Call to Preach," accessed May 29, 2015, *http://www.preachology.com/divine-call.html*.

[17] David Martyn Lloyd-Jones, *Choosing to Preach: A Comprehensive Introduction to Sermon Options and Structures* (Kindle ed.; Grand Rapids, MI.: 2006), 116.

[18] Hollingsworth, "Divine Call."

[19] George W. Peters. *A Biblical Theology of Missions.* (Chicago: Moody, 1972), 278.

[20] Andre M. Rogers, "Am I Called to Preach: Five Biblical Tests," accessed May 29, 2015, *http://ciu.edu/content/am-i-called-preach-five-biblical-tests*

[21] Adapted from Hollingsworth, *Called to Preach.*

[22] Miller, *Preaching*, 61.

[23] Information Adapted from Miller, *Preaching*, Chapter 3.

[24] Andrew Matthew, "An Overview of Contextual Analysis," Lecture, Liberty Baptist Theological Seminary, July 2010.

[25] Matthew, "An Overview."

[26] Kent Spann, "The Main Idea," Lecture, Liberty Baptist Theological Seminary, July 2010.

[27] Spann, "The Main Idea."

[28] Spann, "The Main Idea."

[29] Spann, "The Main Idea."

[30] Spann, "The Main Idea."

[31] Spann, "The Main Idea."

[32] Spann, "The Main Idea."

[33] Murray Lancaster, "Helping Cry," accessed July 13, 2015, *http://luckypennylayne.com/2012/10/29/helping-cry-murray-lancaster/*

[34] Miller, *Preaching*, 44.

[35] *http://www.rd.com/slideshows/readers-digest-trust-poll-the-100-most-trusted-people-in-america/*

36 Ben Awbry, "Illustrations," Working Paper, Midwest Baptist Theological Seminary, 2010.

37 Ben Awbry, "Conclusions," Working Paper, Midwest Baptist Theological Seminary, 2010.

38 Awbry, "Conclusions."

39 Ben Awbry, "Application," Working Paper, Midwest Baptist Theological Seminary, 2010.

40 Awbry, "Application."

41 Awbry, "Application."

42 John Albiston, "Three Steps to Preaching Without Notes," accessed May 29, 2015, *http://www.churchleaders.com/pastors/preaching-teaching/152637-john-albiston-preaching-without-notes.html*

43 Albiston, "Three Steps."

44 Albiston, "Three Steps."

45 Willliam Carl III, "Preaching Tip: Preaching Without Notes," Festival of Homiletics, Posted May 14, 2013, Accessed May 29, 2015, *https://www.festivalofhomiletics.com/blog.aspx?m=4349&post=2578*

46 Carl, "Preaching Tip."

47 Peter E. Roussakis, "Why I Believe in Preaching with a Manuscript," posted January 1, 2001, accessed May 29, 2015, *http://www.preaching.com/resources/articles/11565728/*

48 Roussakis, "Why I Believe."

49 Roussakis, "Why I Believe."

50 Roussakis, "Why I Believe."

51 Lloyd-Jones, *Choosing*, 130.

52 Robert L. Waggoner, "How the Bible Distinguishes Between Preaching and Teaching," accessed May 29, 2015, *http://www.biblicaltheism.com/0402biblicaldistinction.htm*

53 Waggoner, "How the Bible."

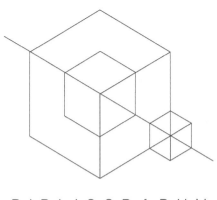

BIBLIOGRAPHY

Albiston, John. "3 Steps to Preaching Without Notes." Accessed May 29, 2015. http://www.churchleaders.com/pastors/preaching-teaching/152637-john-albiston-preaching-without-notes.html

Anderson, Kenton C. *Choosing to Preach: A Comprehensive Introduction to Sermon Options and Structures.* Kindle ed. Grand Rapids, MI: Zondervan, 2006.

Awbry, Ben. " Application." Working Paper. Midwestern Baptist Theological Seminary, 2010.

-----. "Conclusions." Working Paper. Midwestern Baptist Theological Seminary, 2010.

-----. "Illustrations." Working Paper. Midwestern Baptist Theological Seminary, 2010.

Carl, Willliam, III. "Preaching Tip: Preaching Without Notes." Festival of Homiletics. Posted May 14, 2013. Accessed May 29, 2015. https://www.festivalofhomiletics.com/blog.aspx?m=4349&post=2578

Dever, Mark, and Greg Gilbert. *Preach: Theology Meets Practice.* Nashville, TN: B & H Books, 2012.

Lloyd-Jones, David Martyn. *Preaching and Preachers.* 12th ed. Grand Rapids, MI: Zondervan, 1972.

Miller, Calvin. *Preaching: The Art of Narrative Exposition*. Grand Rapids, MI: Baker Books, 2006.

Peters, George W. *A Biblical Theology of Missions*. Chicago: Moody, 1972.

Piper, John. "Advice to Pastors: Preach the Word." February 5, 1996. Accessed May 29, 2015. http://www.desiringgod.org/sermons/advice-to-pastors-preach-the-word

Rogers, Andre M. "Am I Called to Preach: Five Biblical Tests." Accessed May 29, 2015. http://ciu.edu/content/am-i-called-preach-five-biblical-tests

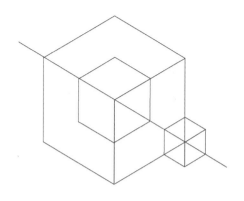

OTHER SUGGESTED READING

Chapell, Bryan. *Christ-centered Preaching: Redeeming the Expository Sermon.* Grand Rapids, MI: Baker Academic, 1994.

Gordon, T. David. *Why Johnny Can't Preach: The Media Have Shaped the Messengers.* Phillipsburg, NJ: P & R Publishing, 2009.

Hamilton, Donald L. *Homiletical Handbook.* Reprint ed. Nashville, TN: B & H Publishing, 1992.

Koller, Charles W.. *How to Preach without Notes.* Combined Paperback ed. Grand Rapids, MI: Baker Books, 1997.

Matthew, Andrew. "An Overview of Contextual Analysis." Lecture. Liberty Baptist Theological Seminary, July 2010.

McDill, Wayne. *The 12 Essential Skills for Great Preaching.* Nashville, TN: Broadman & Holman, 1994.

Robinson, Haddon W. *Biblical Preaching: The Development and Delivery of Expository Messages.* Grand Rapids, MI: Baker Book House, 1980.

Robinson, Haddon W. *The Art and Craft of Biblical Preaching: A Comprehensive Resource for Today's Communicators.* Grand Rapids, MI: Zondervan, 2005.

Roussakis, Peter E. "Why I Believe in Preaching with a Manuscript." Posted January 1, 2001. Accessed May 29, 2015. http://www.preaching.com/resources/articles/11565728/

Spann, Kent. "The Main Idea." Lecture. Liberty Baptist Theological Seminary. July 2010.

Spann, Kent. "The Sermon Idea." Lecture. Liberty Baptist Theological Seminary. July 2010.

Stanley, Andy, and Lane Jones. *Communicating for a Change: Seven Keys to Irresistible Communication.* Sisters, OR: Multnomah, 2006.

Waggoner, Robert L. "How the Bible Distinguishes Between Preaching and Teaching." Accessed May 29, 2015, http://www.biblicaltheism. com/0402biblicaldistinction.htm

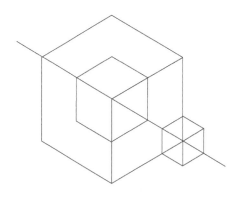

INDEX

Jeff Arnold
On the importance of reading 85
On being yourself 240

Jerry Dean
On the importance of reading 88

Tom Foster
On creativity 179
On staying motivated to preach 182
On compelling conclusions 200

Stan Gleason
On deciding what to preach 100
On sermon preparation 111
On the most important part of the sermon 176
On improving your preaching 263

Scott Graham
On those who influenced him 124
On staying motivated to preach 134
On structuring a sermon for the greatest impact 173
On effective illustrations 186

Ken Gurley
On sermon introductions 162
On preaching from a manuscript 236

Wayne Huntley
On staying motivated to preach 113
On sermon introductions 164
On compelling conclusions 198

Jerry Jones
On improving your preaching 144
On structuring a sermon for the greatest impact 169
On the physical side of passion in preaching 275

Chester Mitchell
On sermon preparation 108
On developing the sermon idea 132
On the importance of prayer 146
On improving your preaching 166

Cindy Miller
On improving your preaching 192
On staying motivated to preach 204
On the most important part of the sermon 213
On being yourself 246

Terry Pugh
On the most important part of the sermon 40
On the high calling of the preacher 67
On improving your preaching 103

Jason Sciscoe
On staying motivated to preach 52
On preaching without notes 222

T. F. Tenney
On those who influenced him 65
On improving your preaching 80
On staying motivated to preach 91
On creativity 177

Janet Trout
On the high calling of the preacher 74
On those who influenced her 238

Joel Urshan
On preaching without notes 220
On improving your preaching 252
On those who influenced him 153
On the importance of prayer 148

Claudette Walker
On improving your preaching 130
On the importance of prayer 149

Raymond Woodward
On improving your preaching 25
On developing the sermon idea 128